D0643447

REVERED AND REVILED

A RE-EXAMINATION OF VATICAN COUNCIL I

JOHN R. QUINN

A Herder & Herder Book
The Crossroad Publishing Company
New York

The Crossroad Publishing Company
www.crossroadpublishing.com

Printed in the United States of America on acid-free paper.

The text of this book is set in 12/15 Adobe Garamond Pro.
Composition by Rachel Reiss.

Library of Congress Cataloging-in-Publication Data
available upon request.

978-0-8245-2329-9

CONTENTS

FOREWORD

by

Cardinal Blase Cupich

Archbishop of Chicago

Revered and Reviled: Vatican I is the final volume in a trilogy of scholarly works Archbishop John Quinn began shortly after he resigned as archbishop of San Francisco in 1995. His aim in this series was to shed light on the Church's tradition and practice as it relates to the exercise of the Petrine ministry of the Bishop of Rome. Quinn's initial motivation was the invitation of Pope John Paul II in *Ut Unum Sint,* which called on Church leaders to help him "find a way of exercising the primacy, which while in no way renouncing what is essential to its mission, is nonetheless open to a new situation" (UUS, 95). Like John Paul II, Archbishop Quinn appreciated the ecumenical significance of taking up this task, which is evident in the progression of his books. In this regard, perhaps one of the most important contributions in this book is the clarity he brings to the specifically delimited nature of the subjects which can be taught in an infallible manner.

Quinn's writings reveal him to be a man constitutionally inclined to meticulous scholarship, but also blessed with decades of experience as a pastor and national leader in the Church. This combination allows him to retrieve the past in a way that helps us better understand the present. That hermeneutical approach of addressing current issues of the day through lessons of the past is on full display in this book.

For instance, Quinn relates his research of the Vatican I discussions about papal primacy and infallibility to the ecclesial issues of today. The Council Fathers, he observes, vigorously debated and prevailed in preserving in the final documents a proper understanding of diocesan bishops as successors of the apostles. This serves as a corrective to the misconception, still present even today, that Vatican I understood the pope as the bishop of all the churches and the local bishop as little more than a "branch manager." In fact, Quinn concludes, "the [Vatican I] Council is not an obstacle to a more collegial exercise of the primacy or an obstacle to the stated intention of Pope Francis for synodality as the way of the Catholic Church."

Likewise, in his treatment of the erroneous "tendency to separate the Pope from the episcopate as above and outside," Quinn points to two significant deficiencies. The theologians and Church leaders who failed to pay sufficient attention to the Fathers of the Church, he explains, tended to lack both an historical consciousness and a proper understanding of the development of doctrine. Here he challenges contemporary Church scholars and leaders to learn from such mistakes and pursue a theological method marked by integrity: "Perseverance in truth requires a knowledge of history and of doctrinal development," he writes.

This method is also evident in Quinn's consideration of the role of conscience, and the danger of an integralist approach that attempts to reduce everything to a dogma of the faith or provides simplistic answers to complex issues.

Of course, no one who knew John Raphael Quinn could be surprised that his writings show such nuance and balance. His probity, integrity and charity led his fellow bishops to rely greatly on his leadership, and for popes to entrust him with matters of great weight and delicacy. His insights are those of a churchman who has not only studied the relationship between papal primacy and episcopal collegiality in theory, but who has lived them over decades of church leadership. This book, his final work, is a fitting epitaph for a man who spent a lifetime serving the Church in the United States, and indeed the global church, with unswerving dedication, insight, and love.

INTRODUCTION

Several years ago, I was struck by words in a lecture given at the Vatican by Michael J. Buckley, S.J., who said, "The way *Pastor aeternus* has been distorted in its reading has influenced ecclesiology for almost one hundred years."[1] Like many, including bishops and priests, I had only the most elementary knowledge of Vatican I and found Father Buckley's statement astonishing. This impelled me to look at the question of the distortion of Vatican I and to examine its history.

I write this book for the moderately educated reader who wishes to have a deeper knowledge of the important issues of papal primacy and of the infallible teaching magisterium of the Pope. My chief aim is to shed light on just what Vatican I did and did not in fact teach about these issues. The rather general belief that the Pope by reason of the primacy must govern all aspects of church life all over the world and that he is infallible in almost all his public teachings does not tally with what the Council actually taught. My objective is to uncover the authentic doctrine on these issues as it was proclaimed by Vatican I and thereby to establish that the Council is not an obstacle to a more collegial exercise of the primacy or an obstacle to the stated intention of Pope Francis for synodality as the way of the Catholic Church.

In doing this work I have relied on Father Giacomo Martina, S.J., the principal modern biographer of Pope Pius IX, the Pope of the Council, as my main source of information. The three-thousand page work of Martina is rich in documentation and abundant in

---

1. Michael J. Buckley, S.J., *Papal Primacy and the Episcopate* (New York: Crossroad, 1998), 45. *Pastor aeternus* are the opening words of the Vatican I decree on papal primacy and infallibility.

its information about Vatican Council I. The work of Dom Cuthbert Butler, OSB, *The Vatican Council 1869–1870,* published in 1962, remains an important and respected source on the subject of the Council. I am indebted to other sources as well who are mentioned in the text.

I must admit that working on this book, I found the study of Vatican I fascinating. I hope the reader may have the same experience. I also found the study illuminating, given the widespread and general exaggerations, both positive and negative, about Pius IX himself and about the teaching of the Council. Finally, I hope that the reader may see the Pope and the Council in a more balanced way. The philosophers said that virtue is the middle point between extremes, between too much and too little. I offer what I have written on Vatican I as a hopefully moderate, balanced and factual account.

My first thanks must go to Francis A. Sullivan, S.J., former Dean of Theology and Professor of Ecclesiology at the Gregorian University in Rome. Father Sullivan carefully read the manuscript, made detailed observations about it, and pointed me to sources I might otherwise have overlooked. I have no truly adequate way of expressing my thanks to him. The author of the modern magisterial work on Cardinal Newman, Ian Ker of Oxford, very generously read my chapter on Newman enabling me to benefit from his comments and scholarship. I must also thank Bishop Robert McElroy of San Diego, who read the manuscript and gave me wise advice. I am grateful to Monsignor Lawrence Purcell of San Diego; Wade and Jane Hughan of San Francisco; and Father Milton Walsh for their observations on the writing of the manuscript. I also express my thanks to the Religious of the Sacred Heart, friends for sixty years, whose unflagging interest in my work and whose prayers have encouraged me to persevere in moments of despair when I thought I would never finish. My special thanks go to Linda Asti, my secretary, who patiently assisted me through the more than five years of my work on this project. I am very grateful also to David Kriegh and library staff at Gellert Memorial Library, St. Patrick's Seminary

Chapter I

NO OTHER VOICE: THE BUILDUP TO A NEW FOCUS ON PRIMACY AND INFALLIBILITY

To understand Vatican Council I, we must go back seventy years to the French Revolution, where the factors which ultimately led to the Council were beginning to take shape. "There can scarcely have been any event in history that was so important in laying the groundwork for the ultimate victory of the papacy at Vatican I as the French Revolution of 1789."[1]

The Revolution heralded a growing social disarray, which only increased in the decades that followed: the Industrial Revolution, the anti-clerical and anti-religious movements spreading over Europe, the Napoleonic wars, and the profound changes brought about by the Congress of Vienna in 1815. The increasing disappearance or modification of absolute monarchies and the new emphasis on the rights of the individual and on freedom of conscience brought the legal recognition of freedom of religion, the secularization of marriage and education, and the legalization of divorce.

Alongside the political and social upheaval, there was a growing storm in the world of ideas, which was tremendously influenced by the Enlightenment.[2] The existence of a personal God, the immortality of the soul, the divinity of Christ—all were being

1. Klaus Schatz, *Papal Primacy From Its Origins to the Present* (Collegeville, Minnesota: Liturgical Press, 1996), 445.

2. See Ulrich Im Hof, *The Enlightenment* (Oxford: Blackwell Publishers, 1994).

called into question. There were challenges to the traditional understanding of the Bible raised by new discoveries of archeology and paleontology and by the critical analysis of biblical texts impelled by the growing knowledge of ancient languages and cultures. Ernest Renan had taken an interest in these studies and spent time in Lebanon and the Middle East, producing a work, *The Life of Christ,* which went through many editions and provoked strong reaction because of its presentation of Christ as a mere human being. It was in this tumultuous social and ideological context, along with the weakened episcopates, that people came to see the Pope as the only power they could turn to as the voice of truth to defend their basic religious beliefs and to defend the permanence and sacredness of marriage and religious education for their children.

Given the situation as they now experienced it, many convinced believers abhorred the disappearance of the *ancien regime,* the monarchy with its union of church and state, where the state upheld the religious and moral teachings of the church in such ways as, for example, the indissolubility of marriage. They thus condemned the democratic state which, in their situation, they experienced as inimical to the church and to the pivotal institutions of society such as marriage and the religious education of children. France thus became the stage on which the buildup to Vatican I took place. Sincere French Catholics understandably interpreted the atheistic strains of the Revolution and its slogan *liberté, fraternité, egalité* (freedom, brotherhood, equality) as hostile to basic values they held dear.

The overthrow of the Church by the powers of the Revolution took place in stages, involving the seizure of church property, the suppression of religious houses and religious vows, and the dispersal of its members. But the major breach between the Church and the Revolution came with the civil constitution of the clergy. This was in effect the creation of a French national church. The National Assembly demanded that the clergy take an oath of allegiance to this new church, although more than half refused to do so. They could not and would not deny the necessity of communion with the Successor of Peter. Some went into exile, to England,

Belgium, to the Papal States or to other countries. "In all, 30,000 clergy fled abroad."[3] Some went to prison. 223 priests, including an archbishop and two bishops, were murdered in the Parisian prisons. Large numbers were left to die in indescribable misery on ships as they awaited deportation.[4] The creation of a state church, together with the execution and deportation of those who refused to take the oath, led to serious divisions within the Church in France.

At the political level, when Napoleon came to power in 1799 as First Consul, he saw that he had to resolve these severe divisions in the nation. His experience both in North Italy and in France made him see the usefulness of religion for public order and civic harmony.[5] "Bonaparte was an able politician for whom religion was an instrument of public policy."[6] He also feared that Catholic Austria, by posing as the champion of religion against atheism, might use the existence of a constitutional church in France as a pretext for possible military intervention against the country. But in reality, what could he do to repair the situation? One obvious solution would be to simply dissolve the constitutional church and return to the *status quo ante*. But it was not so simple. Devout Catholic people would not accept bishops and priests whom they judged to have renounced the faith by taking the oath. Further, bishops and priests who had suffered exile, imprisonment and whose colleagues had been executed could not easily be induced to welcome back into their ranks those who had avoided exile and prison by embracing the constitutional church. Some of these bishops and priests had married. It was not practical to recover public peace simply

---

3. Owen Chadwick *The Popes and European Revolution* (Oxford: Clarendon Press, 1981) 448.

4. A celebrated execution is that of the sixteen Carmelite Nuns of the monastery at Compiegne, which is recounted in the book by William Bush, *To Quell the Terror* (Washington, D.C.: ICS Publications, 1999). These nuns are the subject of Poulenc's opera *Dialogues des Carmélites.*

5. John Martin Robinson, *Cardinal Consalvi* (London: Bodley Head, 1987) 65.

6. Chadwick, *The Popes and European Revolution*, 489.

by dissolving the constitutional church. In addition, Napoleon wanted to reduce the number of dioceses in France. But it was clear that such an action taken unilaterally by the government would never be accepted by Rome and would not be accepted by French Catholics. Consequently, Napoleon's only path forward had to involve the Pope, Pius VII. The "revolutionary general... could not reunite France except by using a Pope whom he despised."[7]

And so, Napoleon, passing through Vercelli in Italy at the head of his army, asked its bishop, Cardinal Martiniana, to notify the Pope of his wish to address the religious situation in France.[8] The Pope responded to this by sending a representative to Paris to begin negotiations, a Monsignor Spina, whom Napoleon had met, and whom he asked for by name. The Pope's aim, as this process began, was "to hold out for the rights of the Church, including the sole direction of seminary education of the clergy, the freedom of religion from any police control, and the right of the pope to correspond with the local clergy[9] free from any state interference."[10] He was also "determined that Napoleon should declare Catholicism to be the official religion of France."[11]

The meetings of Spina with Napoleon's representative, Bernier,[12] were the beginning of the process of drafting the French concordat[13] as a way to resolve the problem. Spina was diffident and slow in moving forward. After some months with no substantial progress, Napoleon's patience was running out. Spina was removed and the Secretary of State, Cardinal Consalvi himself, went to Paris to carry on the negotiations. Napoleon gave him five days

---

7. Chadwick, *The Popes and European Revolution*, 489.
8. Robinson, *Cardinal Consalvi*, 66.
9. The word *clergy* here means the bishops.
10. Robinson, *Cardinal Consalvi*, 66.
11. Robinson, *Cardinal Consalvi*, 66.
12. Bernier had refused to take the oath but was used by Napoleon in this negotiation of the concordat and afterward was made Bishop of Orleans.
13. A Latin word meaning pact or agreement.

to complete the work.[14] Consalvi and Bernier worked tirelessly, sometimes through the night, and eventually produced a mutually-agreed form of the concordat. But when the time came for Consalvi to sign it, Napoleon had changed the final version and inserted points of his own which had not appeared in any of the drafts seen previously by Consalvi. Napoleon thought that Consalvi would sign the document without reading it. But the Cardinal did in fact read it and refused to sign, which created a crisis, since Napoleon had already published his version in the press. But Consalvi stood his ground and refused to sign a concordat which he knew the Pope would not accept. Napoleon, taken aback, grudgingly agreed to allow one more day of negotiations. The main points on which Consalvi insisted were that there should be free and public exercise of religion and a clear statement that the police would not control religion. Consalvi devised wording which Napoleon ultimately accepted: "The Catholic religion, apostolic and Roman, shall be freely exercised in France. Its practice shall be public in conformity with any police regulations which the government shall judge necessary for public order."[15] While this satisfied Napoleon because there was mention of the police, the wording actually limited police control to such things as outdoor processions, "implying that the Church itself was not subject to police control. It ruled out state interference in the organization of seminaries, for instance, or communications with Rome."[16] Having signed the document containing these provisions on July 15, 1801, Consalvi returned to Rome to secure the Pope's signature. The Pope signed it on August 15 and it was taken by courier back to Paris.

Before Consalvi got into the negotiations, there had been several points of major tension. Notable among them was Napoleon's insistence that the Pope remove all the bishops, reduce the number

14. Robinson, *Cardinal Consalvi*, 67.

15. Robinson, *Cardinal Consalvi*, 71.

16. Robinson, *Cardinal Consalvi*, 71.

of dioceses and realign diocesan boundaries. He also wanted to propose candidates for the new bishops himself.

Both Pius VII and Secretary of State Consalvi were reluctant to remove the bishops and rearrange or suppress dioceses. Rome had never removed the episcopate of an entire country. And it was not Rome's practice to suppress dioceses without consultation with the bishops. When Consalvi was in Paris working on the concordat, he pointed out to Napoleon that removal of an entire episcopate would be something new for the Pope. "Ironically, it was Napoleon's insistence on this piece of administrative convenience which was later to open the way for the growth of centralized papal control over local churches and the ultramontane revival," [17] which in turn led to a previously-unknown focus on and devotion to the person of the Pope. The Pope also found it repugnant to remove those bishops who, at great personal cost, had remained in communion with Rome and refused to take the oath. Yet in the end he did so. Why? The Pope ultimately went along with Napoleon on this issue because he was worried that Napoleon might follow the example of Henry VIII of England and set up a schismatic national church. This fear was not groundless, since Napoleon, while at a formal meeting at the Tuileries, surrounded by his ministers and ambassadors, shouted at Consalvi, "Ah, well, Monsieur le Cardinal, you want a schism. So be it. I have no need of Rome... I have no need of the pope. If Henry VIII, who did not have a twentieth part of my power, could change the religion of his own country, the more so can I. In changing the religion of France I will change that of all Europe, everywhere that my power and influence extends."[18] And so by an act of papal primacy unprecedented in history, and with a view to saving the Church in France and in the rest of Europe, Pius VII called for the resignation of the entire French episcopate, redrew the boundaries of dioceses, suppressed some dioceses altogether

---

17. Robinson, *Cardinal Consalvi*, 69.

18. Robinson, *Cardinal Consalvi*, 70.

and regularized the marriages of priests, but not of bishops, who had married.[19]

Another point of contention in the preparation of the concordat was the actual naming of the new bishops. Napoleon insisted on presenting the names himself. He claimed that the power of presenting candidates which the King had enjoyed before the Revolution had passed on to him and to the new government. Here again the Pope was reluctant, but, weighing the possibility that Napoleon might create a schismatic church, he accepted this condition.

As mentioned, the concordat reached Rome in August of 1801. The Pope signed it at once and returned it to Napoleon, who was in Paris. But there was growing uneasiness in Rome when, for nearly eight months, there was complete silence, until Easter of 1802.

The uneasiness turned into astonishment and dismay when Napoleon finally published the text of the concordat in the press. It contained provisions which had not been in the original, which the Pope had signed, provisions he had never seen and to which he had not agreed. He felt tricked. As it turned out, in 1801 Napoleon had not brought the Council of State into the deliberations regarding the concordat and sent his version for the Pope's signature without the knowledge of the Council.[20] When the Council finally saw the document, they exclaimed that Napoleon had conceded too much and demanded additions, called the "Organic Articles"[21] which would give the government greater power over the Church in France. The Organic Articles included, among other things, the main points of Gallicanism, about which more will be said later.

Two factors in this episode, which took place at the beginning of Napoleon's power and clearly contrary to his intentions, highlighted

---

19. Felice Cappello, S.J., *Tractatus canonico-moralis de Sacramentis,* vol.5, *De Matrimonio* (Turin: Marietti, 1952) #442, p. 424. Talleyrand, once Bishop of Autun, was among the bishops whose marriages the Pope refused to validate.

20. Robinson, *Cardinal Consalvi*, 72.

21. They were called *organic* because they had to do with the organization and attributes of the church in France.

papal authority. The first was the concordat itself. The system of concordats did not widely exist prior to the French Revolution. It was the ending of the pre-Revolution union of church and state and the rise of pluralist parliamentary or democratic states and freedom of religion which led to Rome's practice of formal agreements with governments regarding the rights of the Catholic Church in the nation. It is quickly evident that concordats between the government and the Pope strengthened the papal role and Roman centralization, while it diminished the role of the national episcopate, because concordats were between Rome and the government, not between the bishops and the government. This is particularly ironic because Napoleon thought and continued to think that he was using a weak and compliant Pope for his purposes, when in fact what he did only strengthened papal power and authority.

A second factor serving to raise the prestige of the Pope was the removal of the entire French episcopate and the wholesale rearrangement of dioceses in France. This was a stunning and unprecedented exercise of papal primacy and it took place seventy years before the primacy decree of Vatican I. It thus showed that the primacy of the Pope was accepted in the Church well before Vatican I.

The impact of the concordat and the removal of the French episcopate, in addition to enhancing the prestige of the Pope, dealt a mortal blow to French Gallicanism. As mentioned above, the Organic Articles inserted into the concordat included the principles of Gallicanism. The term has had various forms over time, ranging from extreme to moderate. Usually, though, Gallicanism is identified as the theological position which was articulated in 1682 at a national meeting of the French clergy. It comprised four points. The first denied that the Pope had any authority to depose civil rulers or any authority in temporal affairs. The second affirmed that a general council is superior to the Pope. The third asserted that the exercise of papal authority is to be regulated by canon law and, in France, by the laws and customs of the gallican church. The fourth held that the teaching of the Pope is not irreformable without the consent of the church. Gallicanism, as the four points show, was in reality a form of episcopalism—a position which staked out a strong role for the bishops over against the Pope. But the situation in France following on the Revolution made it plain that the bishops of France, in that situation, were incapable of dealing with the problems of the church, leaving the only solution in the hands of the Pope. And some of the bishops who refused to take the oath for the Civil Constitution of the Clergy, refused precisely because they came to see that the Catholic Church could not be separated from the Bishop of Rome. Gallicanism died not only because it was unworkable, as it proved to be in the French situation, but also because it was erroneous as a doctrine. And so the effective end of Gallicanism was another factor which strengthened the role of the papacy in the seventy years before Vatican I.[22]

There was a second set of issues which arose in the years following the concordat. Napoleon had grand, expansive ambitions and imagined himself as the second Charlemagne, bringing all of Europe under his reign. At the same time, he saw that he could not fulfill these ambitions regarding Italy for as long as there were the Papal States with their ruler, the Pope, outside his control. Napoleon's efforts to subordinate the Pope to his control once again had an effect which Napoleon did not foresee, of greatly raising the prestige of the Pope, because, as time passed, he became one of the few leaders in Europe who was willing to stand against Napoleon. This made a strong impression in many circles and is one factor which gave rise to the ultramontane belief that the Pope was the only one capable of standing against the intrusions of civil authorities into the life of the Church and, ultimately, the only voice capable of taking an effective moral stand in the tempestuous welter of the new ideas of the modern world. Thus the decline of good relations between the Pope and Napoleon began when Napoleon

22. A similar event showing the need for papal authority happened in Germany after the secularization of 1803, when there was a need to reorganize the boundaries of dioceses. See Schatz, *Papal Primacy from Its Origins to the Present*, 146–147.

invited the Pope to come to Paris to crown him as Emperor, thereby invoking the memory of Charlemagne, who had been crowned by the Pope on Christmas Day in Rome in the year 800. After weighing the pros and cons, Consalvi advised the Pope to go, on the grounds that Napoleon had restored the Church in France and that by going personally, the Pope might persuade Napoleon to rescind the Organic Articles of the concordat, as well as to force the constitutional bishops make a formal act of submission to the Holy See, something that they had not done. But none of this happened. "The emperor refused to repeal the Organic Articles or to do anything about the constitutional clergy... Thereafter a steady decline set in as Consalvi started to resist Napoleon's aggressions."[23]

But Napoleon was not content with settling the church-state problems just in France. He aimed at a total European domination.[24] He would not tolerate any country taking an independent political line. The cause of the break came when the French occupied the port of Ancona in the Papal States to prevent its use by the English fleet. The Pope refused to accept this, demanding that France immediately vacate Ancona, which Napoleon refused to do. Next Napoleon introduced the Civil Code, including divorce, into northern Italy at his coronation as King of Italy and went on to occupy Civitavecchia, the principal papal port on the west coast. It was obvious that Napoleon was gradually showing his power to crush papal rule completely if he chose to do so. "It was intolerable for Napoleon, when he dominated the whole Italian peninsula, to have in the middle of it a little state which was not part of his system, which did not obey his laws, which allowed the English fleet to visit its ports."[25] Further actions of the Pope angered Napoleon: he refused to recognize Napoleon's brother as King of Naples and refused to annul the marriage of another brother, Jerome, to an American actress.

---

23. Robinson, *Cardinal Consalvi*, 80.

24. Robinson, *Cardinal Consalvi*, 80.

25. Robinson, *Cardinal Consalvi*, 84.

It was not a complete surprise, then, when the first major action against the Pope came when he was made a prisoner in the Quirinal, the papal residence in Rome. Then, on May 17, 1809, "Napoleon published a decree that the remainder of the Papal States were to become part of his empire and Rome was to be an imperial city."[26] With this, the Pope signed the decree of excommunication. Not long afterward, a French general "decided on his own initiative to kidnap the pope and send him to France."[27] This was July 6, 1809, the beginning of a five-year imprisonment of Pius VII. At this point, the Pope was taken to Savona in Italy and "(t)he papal government was dismantled, the cardinals and archives taken to France."[28] The Pope, who was earlier criticized for being weak and was even called "the imperial chaplain" after he agreed to preside at the coronation of Napoleon, was now the object of growing admiration for his stolid resistance to Napoleon.

To all appearances, the Pope, now a prisoner who was incommunicado at Savona, was completely powerless. But that was not the case. Napoleon had, as we saw, persuaded the Pope to grant him the prerogative of presenting candidates for the office of bishop. But now a prisoner in Savona, the Pope refused to approve any such candidates on the basis that he was not free and did not have his advisors at hand. Napoleon tried various expedients to get around this by getting the local authorities, such as cathedral chapters, to elect the bishops as vicars capitular, so they could govern, but without the canonical role as diocesan bishop. These plans were not altogether successful and Napoleon became increasingly angry, leading him to a new plan. He felt that the Pope would succumb if he himself personally exerted pressure on him. He ordered the Pope to be brought to France where he would be closer to Napoleon. Fontainebleau was chosen because it was near Paris, but not close enough to allow large demonstrations by his supporters,

26. Robinson, *Cardinal Consalvi*, 86.

27. Robinson, *Cardinal Consalvi*, 86.

28. Robinson, *Cardinal Consalvi*, 87.

which might have happened if the Pope were in Paris. Yet even though he was a prisoner, the Pope continued to refuse to bow to Napoleon. This steadfast resistance, which no other leader showed, was an important act which immensely raised the respect for and prestige of the Pope.

Another factor in this pre-council period which contributed powerfully to the strengthening of the Pope was ultramontanism. This term described Catholics who came together around the idea that Catholics in Northern Europe had to look "beyond the mountains," the Alps, to Rome to find the voice of truth and divine teaching in the developing social and ideological chaos of that period. People were grieved and distraught by the long years of upheaval and confusion. The bishops were beleaguered and divided and unable to take hold of the situation. People longed for an anchor. They found it in the Pope, who stood firm against Napoleon and who spoke forthrightly and clearly about the new attacks on the faith in the world of ideas.

There were two forms of ultramontanism, the one, more moderate, based on what was taught by St. Robert Bellarmine in the sixteenth century, the other, more extreme, which developed in France and some other countries in the wake of the French Revolution. Bellarmine's position was that the government of the church is a monarchy in the sense that the Pope has supreme power to teach and govern the Church. But Bellarmine also postulated that councils are necessary because the Pope is obligated to take the ordinary and reasonable means to identify revealed truth, and that was not possible without taking into account the faith of the whole church. For Bellarmine, then, there was an infallibility of the church, and the infallibility of the Pope was located within the church, not outside and above the church. Bellarmine's position was taught in the Roman schools from the sixteenth century on and emerged as the formal teaching on infallibility at Vatican Council I in 1870.

The more extreme form of ultramontanism developed primarily, though not exclusively, in France in the years following the Revolution. There was a growing focus on the person of the Pope as the only voice and the only power of good, truth and stability in either the Church or the world. This form of extreme ultramontanism, beginning after 1820, was promoted chiefly by educated lay people who were not educated in theology, who knew little about the history of the Church and the conciliar and collegial structures of the first millennium, and most of whom were either converts to the Catholic Church like Henry Edward Manning in England, or who had recovered their faith after a lapse into unbelief.[29] In France, the most important leaders of this movement were Joseph DeMaistre and Louis Veuillot. Thomas Hobbes, the English political philosopher, a strong promoter of political absolutism or sovereignty, had a substantial influence on DeMaistre.[30] DeMaistre had been French ambassador to Russia for some years. In 1819 he published a widely-read book on the papacy promoting ultramontane ideas. Veuillot was publisher of a newspaper called *L'Univers.* In the English speaking world, a prominent lay promoter of extreme ultramontanism was William G. Ward, editor of *The Dublin Review.*

Another major influence on the growth of extreme ultramontanism was a work which slightly pre-dated DeMaistre, a book written by an Italian monk, Mauro Cappellari, which was published in 1799. The book was entitled *The Triumph of the Holy See and of the Church.* In some ways it was an ironic title because that same year Pope Pius VI, anything but triumphant, was arrested at the age of 82 and brought over the Alps to France, where he died from exhaustion and the rigors of the trip at Valence, 65 miles south of Lyons. He was buried at Valence as Citizen Braschi.

Cappellari's title was also ironic because in 1799, and for several decades thereafter, there was a fairly widespread belief in the secular world that papal authority was finished. "For most authors in Germany and France between 1800 and 1820 the 'papal system' and especially papal infallibility were regarded as passé and matters

---

29. Schatz, *Papal Primacy from Its Origins to the Present*, 147–148.

30. Hermann J. Pottmeyer, *Towards a Papacy in Communion* (New York: Crossroad Publishing Company, 1998), 79.

of only historical interest..."[31] The Cappellari book was ahistorical, rejecting any need to consult history or even the previous teaching of the Church. All that was necessary to understand the Church, according to Cappellari, was what it is at the present time, since what is now always has been, and always will be. Thus he gave little attention to tradition.

Cappellari was the first to conceive primacy of jurisdiction as sovereignty.[32] Sovereignty means absolute and indivisible, that is, sovereign authority cannot be shared and it is the final point of appeal. Cappellari's position, then, had no place for history, the testimony of previous Councils was unnecessary, and the Pope was all sufficient. "It now appeared superfluous to discuss whether the consent of the church, the advice of the cardinals, or the cooperation of the episcopal college must play a part in papal decisions," and "the conception of papal authority as sovereignty became one of the central ideas of the ultramontane movement."[33] "He thus carried to an extreme the paradigm that dominated in the second millennium and annulled the first millennium's justified concern to respect the authority of tradition."[34] This growing tendency to understand the papal office as sovereignty explained an increasing tendency to regard the bishops as field managers or surrogates of the Pope. Papal sovereignty excluded any participation. And so it clearly excluded collegiality.

Cappellari's book was much more widely read after the author was elected Pope as Gregory XVI in 1831, the last Pope not a bishop at the time of his election.[35] It is easy to imagine why such a book, with its triumphant evocations and despite its theological and historical weakness, would appeal to sincere believers, particularly

31. Schatz, *Papal Primacy from Its Origins to the Present*, 144.

32. Pottmeyer, *Towards a Papacy in Communion*, 78.

33. Pottmeyer, *Towards a Papacy in Communion*, 53.

34. Pottmeyer, *Towards a Papacy in Communion*, 52.

35. Gregory XVI was also the last Pope to be a member of a religious order until the election of Pope Francis in 2013.

those who were ignorant of or dismissed history and conciliar or doctrinal tradition in chaotic and troubled times. Here it is important to note that this growth of the understanding of the papal office as sovereignty was in reality the appropriation by the Church of contemporary civil forms and structures into the Church, forms and structures which adversely affected traditional forms and structures. There is a measure of irony here in that the Church was moving toward a stronger appropriation of sovereignty at the time when the secular powers were moving away from it, moving toward more participatory, democratic forms of government.

Three factors, then, conspired to intensify focus on the Pope and prepare the way for Vatican Council I: the spectacular removal of the whole French episcopate, the steadfast resistance of Pius VII to Napoleon, and the rise of the extreme ultramontane movement. Contributing to this tendency to separate the Pope from the episcopate as above and outside was the lack of attention to or knowledge of the Fathers and the Councils, and a narrow focusing on the present as paradigmatic. This absolutizing of the present and lack of historical consciousness brought with it a darkening of any understanding of the development of doctrine. What is always has been and always will be. Yet Newman was to say of himself, "I never should have been a Catholic, had I not received the doctrine of the development of dogmas."[36]

But the irony is that Napoleon, in his treatment of Pius VII, imagined that he was using a weak Pope and that he would bring the papacy under his control. The very means by which he sought to do these things turned out in the end only to further strengthen the papacy and to heighten its importance. As all this history deepened in the consciousness of the Church and its bishops, it is not surprising that by 1870 the council would give a central place on its agenda to the role and the prerogatives of the Pope.

---

36. John Henry Newman, *The Letters and Diaries of John Henry Newman*, (Oxford: Clarendon Press, 1973–1977, Vol 25) Letter to Alfred Plummer, 3 April 1871, 25: 308–310.

Chapter II

THE SYLLABUS OF ERRORS: A MAJOR FORCE IN VATICAN I

The doctrinal and philosophical errors mentioned in the previous chapter caused growing concern for the Pope. The very foundations of faith were at stake and the Church could not simply remain silent. After some years of weighing various options, the first major response came in the form of the *Syllabus of Errors*, to which I turn in this chapter, because the *Syllabus* was one of the significant factors which influenced the Council. "In the papacy's intention, this council was to make the 'Syllabus' its own and turn it into dogma, along with the infallibility of the papal magisterium."[1] If that had happened it would have created crises for Catholic citizens in constitutional democracies and it would have created a grave crisis of faith for many believers.

Where did the *Syllabus* originate? The idea of condemning modern errors in a single document first appeared in a synod of the bishops of Umbria, held at Spoleto in November, 1849.[2] The synod was presided over by Cardinal Gioacchino Pecci, Archbishop of Perugia. Thirty years later, he was to become Pope Leo XIII and publish the first great social encyclical, *Rerum Novarum*, on the rights of labor. The bishops at Spoleto were aware of the publication in 1848 of the Communist Manifesto. This perhaps explains the choice of the specific errors the bishops chose to condemn at

1. Pottmeyer, *Towards a Papacy in Communion*, 47.
2. Giacomo Martina, SJ, *Pio IX (1851–1866)*, (Rome: Editrice Pontificia Universiá Gregoriana,, 1986) Vol II, 289–290.

Spoleto: the denial of the necessity of faith, the denial of the obligation to obey legitimate authority, and the denial of respect for the right to private property. It is surprising, though, that the Spoleto synod made no mention at all of issues which were to be so prominent fifteen years later in the *Syllabus*: the church-state issue, religious freedom, and freedom of conscience. The acts of the Synod were sent to the Vatican but nothing more was heard of the Spoleto meeting.[3] Three years later, in 1852, Father Calvetti, editor of the influential journal *Civiltà Cattolica,* published an article recommending that a list of modern errors should be added to the papal document being developed at that time for the definition of the dogma of the Immaculate Conception.[4] A second draft of the doctrinal decree was thus prepared, which included a list of the principal modern errors to be condemned. But the list dealt chiefly with philosophical ideas and German thinkers such as Hegel, and was too abstract and not in touch with the actual social and political situation. Eventually the plan of combining the condemnation of modern errors with the document on the Immaculate Conception was dropped.

After this, nothing of substance happened for six years until, in 1859, Pius IX decided to consult with several people about his continuing concern over modern errors.[5] One was Abbot Gueranger of Solesmes, France. In addition, he turned to Louis Pie, Bishop of Poitiers, who had been a professor in Rome. He also consulted Monsignor Pierre de Ram, Rector of the Catholic University of Louvain, and Johannes von Geissel, Cardinal Archbishop of Cologne, who was a vigorous leader of the ultramontane movement

---

3. Martina, *Pio IX (1851–1866),* Vol II., 289, n.3. During this period, there were many provincial synods which were directly urged by Pius IX. Considering the criticism made in some quarters in recent decades that episcopal conferences erode the authority of Rome, it is interesting that Pius IX himself encouraged these kinds of provincial synods which dealt with doctrinal issues.

4. Martina, *Pio IX (1851–1866),* Vol. II., 290.

5. Martina, *Pio IX (1851–1866),* Vol. II, 293–298.

in Germany.[6] Pie's response was rigid and scholastic, with no reference to the historical or social context in the document. Gueranger's was polemic and spirited. De Ram had a perspective which included the actual social and economic situation of the time, as well as philosophical trends. Pius IX leaned strongly in the direction of Pie. The three responses were combined into a single text of 79 propositions, which left out the more extreme propositions of Gueranger, but also omitted reference to the actual situation and to social issues raised by de Ram. This version—the collated 79 propositions—was essentially a document of abstract principles and, by 1860, it too was abandoned.[7]

A decisive turn of events came when Bishop Olympe Gerbet of Perpignan wrote a letter to his clergy in July, 1860.[8] With the letter he included a list of 85 points of Catholic doctrine. Probably nothing much would have come of this document if the nuncio to Paris, Sacconi, had not sent it to Pius IX. The Pope was instantly captivated by the Gerbet list and had it printed and given to a new commission he had set up to prepare a list of modern errors. The majority of the cardinals opposed using Gerbet, but the Pope was determined, and a new version of condemned propositions based on Gerbet was devised.

Around this time, some 255 bishops were in Rome for the canonization of Japanese martyrs in 1862. They were asked to give their view of each of the propositions in the new draft and to comment on the advisability of such a project. Of the 255, a third were opposed and at least 95 made no response at all. This was 180 bishops in all, a very large proportion of those asked. Clearly the project was not greeted with burning enthusiasm.[9]

---

6. Martina, *Pio IX (1851–1866)*, Vol. II, 292–293. See also Eric Yonke *Cardinal Johannes von Geissel* in *Varieties of Ultramontanism*, Jeffrey von Arx, S.J., (Washington, DC: Catholic University of America Press, 1998), 12–38.

7. Martina, *Pio IX (1851–1866)*, Vol. II, 295–298.

8. Martina, *Pio IX (1851–1866)*, Vol. II, 299.

9. Martina, *Pio IX (1851–1866)*, Vol. II, 310–315.

While Gerbet's document had a very strong influence on Pius IX, two other events reinforced his determination to publish a list of condemned errors. One was a conference held at Malines in Belgium in August, 1863; the other, a conference held the following month in Munich. Charles Montalembert, the famous French author and political figure, was invited to speak at the Malines conference. In fervent and rousing language, he spoke to a crowd of some 3,000 people on the theme of a "free church in a free state." A disciple of Lamennais and Lacordaire, he was convinced that the democratic state and freedom of religion were the most favorable situations for the Catholic Church. He extolled the usefulness for the church of freedom from the state and called the past support for the church by the state "illusory."[10] He also praised freedom of conscience and freedom of worship, and declared that these could be compatible with Catholic doctrine. Commenting on the speech of Montalembert, Owen Chadwick says, "The whole cast of his speech was against absolutism, and he urged the Church not to be afraid of democracy because it would bring it the freedom it must have."[11]

On the 28th of September, 1863, the Munich conference opened. Unlike Malines, it was not focused on church-state issues but on theological questions. In fact, it was a conference of theologians. If Rome was uneasy about the Malines conference, it was more uneasy about Munich. Primarily, Rome was very concerned that this conference had no endorsement of ecclesiastical authority. But it was a speech by Johannes Döllinger[12] which intensified the negative reaction of Rome. Döllinger, one of the chief organizers of the conference, gave a lengthy speech in which he criticized scholas-

10. Martina, *Pio IX (1851–1866)*, Vol. II, 316.

11. Owen Chadwick, *A History of the Popes 1830–1914* (Oxford: Oxford University Press, 2003), 172.

12. Döllinger was a priest and historian. In 1863, the *Syllabus* had not yet appeared. Years later, in 1870, he vigorously opposed the Council on the grounds of lack of freedom and he rejected the decree on infallibility. He was excommunicated after the Council.

tic theology and called for recognition of the proper freedom of theologians in relationship to the magisterium of the Church. But the Munich conference also adopted traditional theological positions when it condemned the rationalist *Life of Jesus* by Renan and addressed a letter to the Pope expressing complete obedience and communion.[13] Pius IX was momentarily reassured by the letter. But persuaded by sources in Germany and in the Curia, he ultimately took a more negative view of the conference. Three months after Munich, the Pope addressed a letter to the German episcopate in which he declared that no such conference should be held in the future without the explicit approval of the hierarchy. He went on to praise the value of the scholastic method in theology, affirmed the authority of the magisterium to watch over and guide Catholic doctrine, and explicitly rejected Döllinger's position that obedience and acceptance were due only to defined dogmas of the faith but did not include the teaching of the ordinary magisterium.[14]

Through the fall and winter of 1863, there were various efforts to induce Rome to issue a condemnation of Montalembert and his push for freedom of religion embodied in the words "a free church in a free state." Aware of this development, the Prime Minister of Belgium, Adolphe Deschamps, addressed a 23-page letter to the Secretary of State, Cardinal Antonelli.[15] He made the point that to condemn Montalembert would be to condemn the modern constitutional state. It would please the enemies of the church and create profound, perhaps insoluble, problems of conscience for Catholics, especially for Catholic politicians in modern constitutional states where there was freedom of religion. The question, he said, was whether Rome should defend the freedom of the church within the framework of civil freedom or whether the church should stand before the world as the enemy of freedom. Deschamps knew that the world would not return to the political situation which existed

13. Martina, *Pio IX (1851–1866)*, Vol. II, 317.

14. Martina, *Pio IX (1851–1866)*, Vol II., 320.

15. Martina, *Pio IX (1851–1866)*, Vol II., 332.

prior to the French Revolution and that the new world was one which would place a high value on freedom. It was not only Belgians and Frenchmen like Dupanloup, Bishop of Orleans, who saw this reality. Some forty years before this, the Secretary of State to Pope Pius VII, Cardinal Consalvi, had compared the French Revolution to the universal biblical flood which was the beginning of an entirely new era for humanity.[16] Yet alongside these efforts to prevent the condemnation of Montalmbert, the Pope was also getting strong pressure from Pie of Poitiers and others to condemn him. Bishop Malou of Bruges wrote to the Pope expressing astonishment that there was such a delay in condemning Montalembert.[17] The increasing focus on Montalembert brought with it a more explicit consciousness of the church-state issue which led to the explosive final propositions of the *Syllabus.*

It was during these months of 1863 that a key figure in the development of the final version of the *Syllabus* entered the scene—Luigi Bilio. Bilio belonged to a small religious order called the Barnabites and taught philosophy and theology in several Italian seminaries. He was intelligent but lacked historical perspective. He tended to read documents apart from their context and never grasped the irreversible culture shift represented by the French Revolution. Like Pius IX, he believed that the old union of Church and State would return and that democracy had no future.[18] The much respected 19th century American scholar, Monsignor James Corcoran, said of Bilio, "... (l)ike too many of the rest, he has never looked boldly in the face of the world in which we live and to which we are coming."[19] His rise began when he was sent to Rome and became a consultor at the Holy Office. He came to the attention of Pius IX when, in that capacity, he prepared a critique of the speeches

16. Martina, *Pio IX (1851–1866)*, Vol II., 327.

17. Martina, *Pio IX (1851–1866)*, Vol II., 326.

18. Martina, *Pio IX (1851–1866)*, Vol II., 327–328, 331.

19. J. J. Hennessy, "James A. Corcoran's Mission to Rome: 1868–1869," *The Catholic Historical Review* 48 (1962–1963): 172.

of Montalembert at Malines. The Pope was impressed by Bilio's negative judgment of Montalembert and he was very pleased that Bilio's paper repudiated Montalembert's ideas on the separation of church and state and on freedom of conscience. And so it was to Bilio that Pius turned to draft the *Syllabus of Errors*. Accordingly, in March, 1864, a new commission was created, made up of some Roman theologians and a few members of the staff of the Holy Office. It was given the charge of preparing a new list of errors to be condemned including the errors contained in Montalembert's speeches. With Bilio as the lead author, the document was ready by June and given to the cardinal members of the Holy Office. Their judgment of this new list of errors was the same as they had expressed in 1862 to an earlier version: the propositions were not well formulated, they did not touch on the principal errors of modern society, and it was not fitting that the Pope should follow so closely a document written by a French bishop to his clergy. Here, of course, the reference is to the list of Gerbet, which Pius IX liked so much and on which Bilio in fact based much of his draft.[20] The cardinals of the Holy Office further explicitly pointed out that the majority of bishops consulted at the time of the canonization of the Japanese martyrs in 1862 were not favorable. But in an effort to find a way to deal with the Pope's obvious determination to publish some condemnation of modern errors, they came up with the suggestion that he publish an encyclical, but in a separate document, a list of modern errors. On August 12, 1864, the Pope approved this plan, and Bilio was given the task of preparing the draft of an encyclical and another revised list of errors.[21]

Bilio went to work and reduced the list of errors to 22 from the original 53. Toward the end of September, the cardinals of the Holy Office approved 20 of the 22 propositions and, the very same day, the Pope accepted their decision and directed Bilio to prepare an encyclical. Bilio produced a draft fairly quickly. The encyclical, an apocalyp-

20. Martina. *Pio IX (1851–1866)*, Vol II., 339.

21. Martina, *Pio IX (1851–1866)*, Vol II., 340.

tic view of modern society and known by its opening words, *Quanta cura,* condemned freedom of conscience and called for recognition of the Catholic Church by the state even to the point of calling on the state to use its power to defend and protect the church.[22]

The more difficult task for Bilio was preparing the list of modern errors. We have seen that the cardinals had approved the list of 20 errors which Bilio presented to them. But what finally emerged was a list of 80 errors, which was, in reality, a new list. What led to the decision to create an entirely new list? The archives do not answer this question, but the conjecture is that it gradually became clear that the 20 approved theses were too much centered on the church-state issue and did not adequately deal with the wider range of modern errors.[23] Ultimately, Bilio had come up with a list of 84 propositions which clearly reflected the earlier work of Gerbet. They were divided into ten sections, ranging from the first, *Pantheism, naturalism and absolute rationalism*, to the final section, containing the last four propositions, *Errors connected with modern liberalism.* This new version was less exclusively focused on church-state issues and included theological and philosophical errors. The individual propositions carried no indication of the level of condemnation. This lack of qualification, together with the lack of any context, reinforced confusion and ambiguity about the meaning of the propositions, leaving them open to distorted interpretations. This is notoriously the case with the condemned proposition 80, which reads, "The Roman Pontiff can and must be reconciled with, and come to terms with, progress, with liberalism and with modern civilization."[24] The proposition as it stood was widely interpreted as portraying the Pope as the enemy of democracy and of modern progress, including technological progress. Butler says, "Some journalists so far lost

---

22. Martina, *Pio IX (1851–1866),* Vol. II, 348.

23. Martina, *Pio IX (1851–1866),* Vol. II, 342.

24. Henricus Denziger and Adolfus Shönmetzer, SJ, *Enchridion Symbolorum* (Barcinone, Frisburgi, Romae: Herder, MCMLXXVI), 584 (author's translation)

their heads as to say the Pope had condemned all the discoveries of modern science and industry, railroads, electric telegraphs, photography . . . together with the steam engine and gas light."[25] In actual fact, proposition 80 was taken from a papal consistorial Address of 1861, which dealt with the struggle the church was having in Italy and other countries where the governments invoked "progress" as an excuse for such things as violating concordats with the Holy See, interference by the state in the internal affairs of the church, preventing bishops from assuming their responsibilities in their dioceses and for expelling the religious orders. These were among the things that were called progress, which, of course, the Pope could not accept.[26] This context, which gives an understandable reason for the Pope's condemnation of government policies, was entirely absent in the text of the *Syllabus* as it stood and led Owen Chadwick to say of proposition 80, "No sentence ever did more to dig a chasm between the pope and modern European society."[27]

Bilio's work when he presented it to the cardinals in Rome consisted of 84 propositions and was ready to be given to the printer. At the last minute, Bilio, anxious about the effect two propositions would have—on his own authority and without the knowledge of the Pope—suppressed propositions 78 and 84 which had to do with the advantages of a constitutional state and with the goals and intentions of the Italian unity movement.[28]

And so, in December of 1864, Cardinal Antonelli, Secretary of State,[29] sent two documents to all the bishops: the encyclical

25. Dom Cuthbert Butler, *The Vatican Council 1869–1870* (Newman Press, Westminster, Maryland, 1962), 54–55

26. A notable example of what the Pope was talking about was Cardinal Filippo Maria Guidi who had been named Archbishop of Bologna in 1863 but was never able to assume his duties there because of government opposition. He died in 1879.

27. Chadwick, *A History of the Popes 1830–1914*, 176.

28. Martina, *Pio IX (1851–1866)*, Vol II, 343–44.

29. Cardinal Antonelli was never a priest or bishop. He was a deacon.

Quanta cura and a second document entitled *Syllabus containing the most important errors of our time which have been condemned by Our Holy Father Pius IX in allocutions, at consistories, in encyclicals and other apostolic letters.* The Syllabus contained 80 errors and with each error there was given a reference to the papal document in which that error had been condemned. These are the condemned errors which caused most spirited reaction:

> #15 *Every man is free to embrace and profess the religion which, led by the light of reason, he thinks is true.*
>
> #55 *The church ought to be separated from the state and the state from the church.*
>
> #77 *In our times it is no longer suitable that the Catholic religion should be the only state religion and exclude all others.*
>
> #78 *And so in some Catholic regions it is laudable the non-Catholic citizens migrating to those countries should all be able to publicly exercise their own religion.*
>
> #79 *It is indeed not true that freedom of worship and freedom to express and publish opinions and beliefs contributes to the moral detriment and to the propagation of the vice of indifference.*
>
> #80 *The Roman Pontiff can and must come to terms with and must reconcile himself with progress, with liberalism and with modern society.*[30]

---

30. Denziger, *Enchridion Symbolorum*, 2977–2980 (author's translation). Liberalism and the adjective *liberal*, used in proposition 80, is language which has undergone great changes over time and is a very complex reality. For a treatment of the topic see Konrad Hecker, *Liberalism and Liberal Theology* in *Sacramentum Mundi*, Vol 3, 304–309, (New York: Herder And Herder, 1969).

When the encyclical and the syllabus became public, there was not only widespread dismay over what was read as a condemnation by the Pope of the separation of church and state and freedom of religion; there was the terrible anguish of conscience for Catholic citizens in democratic countries, and for Catholic politicians, who wondered whether they could obey the civil laws or keep their oath of office in a pluralist democratic society.

Read with care and impartial judgment, many of the propositions of the *Syllabus* would be readily embraced by believers everywhere. For example, all Christian bodies would agree that one should condemn what is affirmed in proposition 6: "The faith of Christ is in opposition to human reason, and divine revelation not only is not useful, but is even hurtful to human perfection." But propositions like this gained little attention. It was the propositions having to do with church-state issues which were the main focus of the explosive public reaction. Here we recall that the cardinals had warned the Pope that "the propositions are not well formulated."

The reaction to the *Syllabus* was so widespread and so strong that the Pope saw that he had to do something to calm the waters.[31] So he called on a theologian to prepare an instruction explaining the correct interpretation of the *Syllabus*, including a statement about how Catholics should apply it in constitutional democracies. The instruction itself was never made public and the identity of the theologian is not known, but it is reasonable to assume that Bilio was the author. The French constitution included religious freedom and so the oath to uphold the constitution meant defending freedom of religion. In the mind of Rome, religious freedom was equivalent to indifferentism, a grave evil.[32] Nevertheless, the theologian, invoking the principle of the lesser evil, wrote that French Catholics could take the oath to avoid worse evils, but they were not to understand the oath as approving religious indifference.

31. Martina, *Pio IX (1851–1866)*, Vol II, 349.

32. Martina, *Pio IX (1851–1866)*, Vol II, 350–52.

This line of reasoning was based on what Pius VII had done in 1804[33] when he was preparing to attend the coronation of Napoleon I. The Pope was severely troubled when he came to see that the Emperor whom he was to crown would have to swear to uphold freedom of religion in France. The solution was that the Pope, by his presence at the coronation, was not endorsing freedom of religion but was tolerating it as a lesser evil. Hence the instruction prepared for Pius IX in the wake of the uproar over the *Syllabus* adopted the approach that the *Syllabus* did not condemn *tolerating* religious freedom in a constitutional state. This is known as the thesis-hypothesis solution, which meant that the ideal would be a Catholic state—the thesis. But where there was a democratic constitutional state, which included freedom of religion, freedom of religion could be tolerated as a practical measure for the sake of public peace and order—the hypothesis.

This kind of practical accommodation was not new to the American bishops. In the last decade of the eighteenth century, the first Catholic bishop in the United States, John Carroll, was vigorous in defending religious liberty as expressed in the first amendment of the Constitution. One biographer says of Carroll, "America's leading Catholic was clearly on record as a proponent of a separation of Church and State," and his brother was a central figure in shaping the first amendment to the Constitution in 1791.[34] And notwithstanding the condemnations in the *Syllabus*, twenty years after its appearance, one of the most distinguished figures of American Catholic history, Cardinal James Gibbons, a participant in Vatican Council I, praised freedom of religion in America in a speech given in Rome on March 25, 1887, when he was made a cardinal. For the most part, bishops in democratic countries recognized the great

---

33. Martina, *Pio IX (1851–1866)*, Vol II, 349 "...they turned at once to the distinction which was a classic one for some eighty years between thesis and hypothesis." (author's translation).

34. Annabelle M. Melville, *John Carroll of Baltimore* (New York: Charles Scribner's Sons, 1955), 89.

benefits to the church deriving from the separation of church and state and from religious freedom.

But the most effective voice in clarifying the meaning of the *Syllabus* was Dupanloup of Orleans. He published a pamphlet on the *Syllabus* pointing out that the 80 propositions were presented as having equal importance and were sweeping and universal statements. Hence, if the meaning of the propositions was to be determined, they had to be read in the context of the original documents from which they had been drawn. When read in the context of the originating documents, the propositions often had a meaning different from that conveyed when they were stated without any background or context. The work of Dupanloup was widely publicized and brought a certain sense of relief to many. He received more than 600 letters from different countries thanking him. Even Pius IX wrote a letter thanking him. Veuillot, in Rome at the time, made vigorous efforts to prevent the Pope from writing the letter to Dupanloup, but the Secretary of State, Cardinal Antonelli, was strongly in favor because, being in direct contact with governments, he grasped the potential harm of the *Syllabus* for the mission of the Church. In his letter, the Pope praised Dupanloup for bringing to light the correct meaning of the *Syllabus* and for refuting its regrettable and calumnious distortions.[35] But Dupanloup's fine work did not ultimately remove the problem or clear the air altogether.[36]

This is borne out by the fact that a respected historian of Vatican I states, "All this business of the *Syllabus* was very much alive during the Council . . ."[37] An early sign of the link between the Syllabus and the Council is that on December 6, 1864, two days before the promulgation of the encyclical and the *Syllabus*, Pius IX revealed for the first time, and in confidence to a small group of cardinals,

35. Martina, *Pio IX (1851–1866)*, Vol II, 353.

36. Martina, *Pio IX (1851–1866)*, Vol II, 356.

37. Butler, *The Vatican Council 1869–1870*, 57.

his firm intention to convoke an ecumenical council.[38] This was certainly an indication that, in the Pope's mind, there was a link between the *Syllabus* and the coming Vatican Council I. It should not be surprising then that at the time of the council itself, many, including some governments, believed that an important aim of the council was to reinforce the condemnations found in the *Syllabus*, especially the condemnation of the separation of church and state and of freedom of conscience. In other words, there was some foundation for the fear that the council would include a condemnation of the modern constitutional state.

Further justification was given to these fears when, ten months before the opening of the Council, in February of 1869, the same *Civiltà Cattolica* article which reported French Catholics as calling for the definition of infallibility by acclamation, called also for the solemn proclamation of the doctrine of the *Syllabus*.[39] In England, Manning was among those who wanted the *Syllabus* defined and who promoted the viewpoint that the Pope was infallible in every kind of official and public statement. After the Council, Newman referred to this movement: "They hoped to get a decree that would cover the Syllabus and they *have* not got it."[40] The publicity given to the possibility that the *Syllabus* would be defined understandably created alarm among the governments. They feared growing problems of public order and civic peace if Catholics were to be obliged to believe that the separation of church and state, freedom of conscience and freedom of religion were condemned infallibly in the Council. The *Syllabus* was not an inconsequential matter. Some historians regard it as a turning-point in the history of the church.[41]

---

38. Martina, *Pio IX (1851–1866)*, Vol II, 347.

39. See Francis A. Sullivan, S.J., *Creative Fidelity* (New York: Paulist Press, 1996), 142. "... many ... looked for a definition that would mean that each error in the Syllabus had been infallibly condemned."

40. John Henry Newman, *Letters and Diaries*, Letter to Lady Simeon, Nov. 1, 1870, 25: 224. The decree which Newman mentions here is the decree on infallibility.

41. Chadwick, *A History of the Popes 1830–1914*, 169.

The confusion created by the *Syllabus* has endured for more than a century. This is attested, for instance, by the fact that it was used against John F. Kennedy when he ran for President of the United States. The *Houston Chronicle*, writing about that campaign, said in an article in 2007, "Kennedy simply had to convince Protestants that he was a good American." And speaking of Kennedy's meeting with Protestant ministers, the article said, "The Protestant ministers had some basis other than residual nativism for their skepticism. Pope Pius IX in 1864 had included certain notions of separation of church and state and religious freedom in his 'Syllabus of Errors.' The long-standing tradition of the Catholic Church was that error has no rights."[42]

As this long history of the *Syllabus* unfolds, it is interesting to see the change that took place in what was to have been its original focus. In the beginning, the focus of the Pope was on theological and philosophical errors of the age. But these really took second place when the *Syllabus* actually became public and the church-state issue emerged as the central concern for public opinion. It all came to a head when the *Syllabus* itself condemned religious freedom and freedom of conscience in propositions 78 and 79, without any context and without any qualifying note. It was this lack of precision and context which, more than anything else, derailed the Pope's personal desire to focus on philosophical and theological errors. Religious freedom and freedom of conscience were realities which everyone understood and which all modern democratic states guaranteed. When these cherished realities were thought to be condemned and the condemnation even said to be infallible by some Ultramontanes, a huge and widespread conflagration ensued that would not end in principle until the coming of the Second

42. Rick Casey, *The Houston Chronicle,* "Why JFK Was Briefer Than Romney," December 7, 2007. The Catholic Church abandoned this approach at Vatican Council II in its decree on Religious Liberty, where it based its position on the dignity of the human person and the dogmatic principle of the freedom of the act of faith.

Vatican Council and its historic decree on religious liberty.[43] That decree, in fact, embraced a truth proclaimed in the decree on faith of Vatican I, that the act of faith is free.[44]

Five years after Vatican I, Newman showed how impossible it was, using any accepted Catholic theological method, to claim that the *Syllabus* was a dogmatic definition. In his *Letter to the Duke of Norfolk*, he points out the fact that the condemnations in the *Syllabus* are not exact quotations from the thirty-two documents, letters, encyclicals and allocutions of Pius IX. "...(W)hen we turn to those documents, which are authoritative, we find that the Syllabus cannot even be called an echo of the Apostolic Voice; for, in matters in which wording is so important, it is not an exact transcript of the words of the Pope, in its account of the errors condemned, – just as is natural in what is professedly an index for reference."[45] And he goes on to say that the Syllabus "intrinsically and viewed in itself, is nothing more than a digest of certain Errors made by an anonymous writer."[46] He concludes, "The Syllabus, then, is a list, or rather an index of the Pope's Encyclical or Allocutional 'proscriptions'...But we can no more accept it as *de fide,* as a dogmatic document, than another index or table of contents."[47]The *Syllabus* admittedly contains some serious defects. But it also has some positive features which deserve recognition. We should not forget or minimize the truth that the main idea behind the *Syllabus* was to take a stand against serious errors touching on truths of divine revelation. The reader has only to

43. Vatican Council II, *Declaration on religious freedom* in *Decrees of the Ecumenical Councils*, Norman P. Tanner, S.J., ed., (Sheed and Ward and Georgetown University Press, 1990), Vol II, 1001–1011.

44. Vatican Council I, *Dogmatic constitution on the catholic faith*, canon 3, Tanner, Vol II, 810. The freedom of the act of faith is further explained in the *Catechism of the Catholic Church, n. 160.*

45. John Henry Newman, *Letter to His Grace the Duke of Norfolk* in*Certain Difficulties Felt by Anglicans in Catholic Teaching,* (Westminster, MD: Christian Classics), Vol II, 1969, 281.

46. Newman, *Duke of Norfolk*, 277.

47. Newman, *Duke of Norfolk*, 283.

think of propositions in the earlier part of the *Syllabus*, such as the condemnation of pantheism, rationalism, or the propositions calling for the subordination of the Church to the State.[48] As it happened, Vatican I did not define the *Syllabus* as Newman so ably showed. But the Council did develop its own much more balanced teaching on some of the doctrinal and philosophical errors of the 19th century in its first formal decree of the Council called *Dogmatic constitution on the Catholic faith.*[49] But none of this made an impression on the public at large because it was proposition 80 that "was to be the only proposition that most of Europe noticed."[50]

The *Syllabus*, then, was a significant influence during the Council, not only because of proposition 80, but because the extreme Ultramontanes such as Manning and Ward were actively promoting the viewpoint that the Pope was infallible in all such public documents and were championing a broad and wide ranging infallibility for the Pope. W. G. Ward of the *Dublin Review* was the prime mover of the extreme English Ultramontanes. He vigorously rejected the idea that infallible pronouncements were few and far between. "For him the eighty propositions of the *Syllabus* were 'beyond question the Church's infallible utterance'; and not only so, but the thirty encyclicals and allocutions from which the propositions were culled were all thereby shown to have been *ex cathedra* in their entirety."[51] He also showed a trait common to the intransigent then and now, "He insisted with uncompromising assurance that his view was the only Catholic one, and must be accepted as the Catholic Faith necessary for salvation, only invincible ignorance excusing from mortal sin."[52] The Council did not embrace this view. Newman rejected it. Vatican Council I did not become the Council of the *Syllabus*.

---

48. Martina, *Pio IX (1851–1866)*, Vol II, 349.

49. Tanner, *Decrees of the Ecumenical Councils*, Vol II, 804–811.

50. Chadwick, *A History of the Popes*, 176.

51. Butler, *The Vatican Council 1869–1870*, 58.

52. Butler, *The Vatican Council 1869–1870*, 59.

Chapter III

THE PRIMACY OF THE POPE

Vatican Council I opened on Wednesday, December 8, 1869, during a torrential rain, with 774 bishops from all parts of the world in attendance.[1] Over the following weeks, some votes were taken on the membership of various commissions, and there was some initial discussion of a document on faith and reason which was sent back to the drafting committee for more work. Then, on January 21, 1870, a draft document on the Church, based on the *Syllabus of Errors*, was distributed to the bishops.[2] Its chief author was Klemens Shrader, professor at the Roman College, who held that the *Syllabus* was a series of dogmatic definitions.[3]

After this first draft was distributed to the bishops, they were given ten days to submit their written observations. A synopsis of these observations compiled from 140 documents submitted to the drafting commission filled 104 pages. One could think that 140 documents coming from a body of more than 700 members would not be very representative, but in fact, many of the 140 documents were joint productions with multiple signatories. The leaders of the minority figure prominently among those contributing to these

1. Martina, *Pio IX (1851–1866)*, Vol III, 166.
2. Yves Congar, *L'Eglise* (Paris: Editions Du Cerf, 1996), 441.
3. Manning had known Schrader when he went to Rome at the time that he became a Catholic priest in 1851. The Gregorian University is the successor of the Roman College.

observations, an early indication that the minority did not feel intimidated in expressing its views.[4]

Weighty criticism of the draft emerged among the bishops on several important points. They said that the document was too academic. A more substantial objection to the draft, however, was that it focused exclusively on the Pope. They pointed out that this was a decree on the Church, yet it contained nothing about the bishops or about ecumenical councils. There was a gnawing concern that the draft's exclusive focus on the Pope isolated him from the episcopate and placed him outside and beyond the bishops. They said that the draft text, which so exalted the Pope, was contrary to the divine constitution of the Church by portraying the bishops as mere vicars of the Pope or field managers, and the Church as a single diocese with a single bishop, the Pope. Among the bishops of the minority there were many who knew the Fathers, the Councils and the history of the Church, particularly during the first millennium. Their concern grew out of the fear that understanding papal primacy as sovereignty was not consonant with history. But a far more substantive objection was that framing primacy in the language of sovereignty as the text did was contrary to the divine constitution of the Church in which both the petrine office and the episcopate are divine institutions.

Accordingly, a second draft on the Church, now divided into two parts, was circulated four months later, on May 9, 1870. Part I, entitled *First dogmatic constitution on the church of Christ,*[5] treated topics relating to the Pope. It consisted of an introduction and four chapters: the primacy of Peter in the New Testament, the continuing of Peter's primacy in the Roman Pontiff, the prerogatives of papal primacy, and a final chapter on infallibility.

---

4. Butler, *The Vatican Council 1869–1870*, 332. Butler also says "After reading through the Observations I am prepared to state that there was not any single case of questioning the primacy in itself or in its implications..." He repeats this again on page 334.

5. Tanner, *Decrees of the Ecumenical Councils*, Vol II, 811.

Part II of the revised document on the Church focused on the role of the bishops. Unfortunately, Part II was never debated or enacted thanks to the abrupt interruption of the Council in July, 1870. In the present chapter, I will review the Introduction and the three chapters on Peter and the primacy of the Pope. In the following chapter, I will address papal infallibility.

The Introduction lays the groundwork for everything that will be said about the primacy in the following chapters by presenting the reasons why Christ established the primacy, that is, to protect and promote communion. The Church as communion is prominent in the very first words of the Introduction which begins, "Pius, bishop..." The Pope identifies himself as a bishop and therefore as a member of the body or college of bishops. He goes on to say explicitly that his teaching is within the college of bishops by stating that it is given "with the approval of the sacred council."[6] Then the reason for the primacy is given: the unity of the Church and of all believers depends on the unity of the episcopate, and the primacy exists to foster and maintain the unity of the bishops on which the unity of the faithful depends. "In order, then, that the episcopal office should be one and undivided and that, by union of the clergy[7], the whole multitude of believers should be held together in the unity of faith and communion, he set blessed Peter over the rest of the apostles and instituted in him the permanent principle of both unities (the episcopate and the faithful) and their visible foundation."[8] The Introduction places the primacy in function of unity in faith and communion. It does not exact uniformity. This is shown, for example, by the fact that the Eastern Churches retain their own canonical, liturgical, theological and spiritual traditions as reiterated in Vatican Council II.[9]

---

6. Tanner, *Decrees of the Ecumenical Councils*, Vol II, 811.

7. The word *clergy* here means the bishops.

8. Tanner, *Decrees of the Ecumenical Councils*, Vol II, 812.

9. *Lumen gentium 23*, Tanner, *Decrees of the Ecumenical Councils*, Vol II, 867–868. See Francis A. Sullivan, S.J. *The Church We Believe In* (Mahwah, NJ: Paulist Press, 1988) 34–65.

From this Introduction, we learn further that the Church is to endure and continue through time, and that therefore the ministry of Peter and the Apostles in the service of unity and communion is to endure so that all believers may be one in faith and communion. The Introduction declares that the teaching of this Council decree on the Church is to be understood "in accordance with the ancient and unchanging faith of the whole church."[10] Thus the subsequent chapters on primacy and infallibility are all situated and to be interpreted in the context of the ancient teaching of the Church and previous councils. This is the same position John Paul II was to adopt in the encyclical *Ut unum sint* in which he used the first millennium as an example and guide for reforming the exercise of the papacy today.[11] Pope John Paul II rightly understood the Vatican I teaching on primacy as situated in the context of the history and structures of the first millennium.

Following the Introduction, the first two chapters of Part I dealt with the Apostle Peter. Both chapters passed without much difficulty, an indication that there was general agreement among the bishops with the teaching of these chapters. Chapter I affirms that a primacy of jurisdiction was immediately and directly promised to Peter and actually conferred on him by Christ. More than any other text, Matthew 16:16–19, "You are Peter, and on this rock I will build my church . . . I will give you the keys of the kingdom of heaven, and whatever you bind on earth shall be bound in heaven, and whatever you loose on earth shall be loosed in heaven," has figured prominently in controversies about the role of Peter in the New Testament, and in late centuries has become the central text used by the Catholic Church for the support of the papacy.[12] This derives from the fact that in Mat-

10. Tanner, *Decrees of the Ecumenical Councils*, Vol II, 812.

11. Pope John Paul II, *Ut unum sint* (Rome: Libreria Editrice Vaticana, May 25, 1995) 55, 56.

12. Raymond E. Brown, John Reumann, eds., *Peter in the New Testament* (Minneapolis: Augsburg Publishing House; New York: Paulist Press, 1973), 83.

thew, Peter is one of the first two disciples to be called by Jesus and is the first in the list of the Apostles, explicitly designated as first (*protos*). In Matthew it is Peter who gets involved when church problems arise. For instance, Peter takes the initiative in asking Jesus for guidance on the subject of the troubling obligation to forgive (18:21–22), on the subject of Jesus' declaration that the disciples are not bound by the Jewish food regulations (15:15) and on the issue of whether the disciples are obliged to pay the Temple tax (18:21–22). Then there is the fact that it was Jesus who gave Simon the new name *Peter* (rock), which foretold the role he would play, who gave him the keys of the kingdom, and who saved Peter when he was sinking. An indicator of a unique status among the other Apostles is that in making his confession "You are the Christ, Son of the living God," Matthew does not present Peter simply as spokesman of the others, but as the recipient of a special divine revelation for which Jesus gives him a special blessing and declares that Peter is the rock on which the Church will be built. Furthermore, it is only to Peter and to none of the others that Jesus says, "I will give you the keys of the kingdom of heaven."[13] There is in Matthew, then, a prominence and a role of Peter both in relationship to Jesus and to the Church which the other Apostles do not have.

A significant Petrine text is found in the Gospel of John. Many scholars believe that John 21 is older than the rest of John's Gospel and therefore its recognition of a unique and central role for Peter reflects a very early period before the written Gospels.[14] In verses 15—17 of John 21, the focus is on Peter, who is given the command "feed my sheep" three times. It is the shepherd who feeds the sheep and so this charge links John 21 with John 10, the chapter on the Good Shepherd. In chapter 10, the Good Shepherd is also described as laying down his life for his sheep, and at the end of chapter 21, there is the prediction that Peter himself

---

13. See Brown, *Peter in the New Testament*, 107

14. See Brown, *Peter in the New Testament*, 139–147

will die the death of a martyr.[15] There is, then, a special link between Peter, the shepherd, and Christ. In imitation of Christ, Peter will die a martyr, laying down his life for the flock. It is also significant that while the other members of the Twelve are called fishermen, Peter has the distinction of being the only apostle who is called to be a shepherd in this Gospel. "Feed my lambs, feed my sheep." (Jn. 21:15–18).

Shepherd was a much-used image for the duties of kingship in the Bible. Commenting on the familiar psalm 23, "The Lord is my shepherd," John Eaton, who has written extensively on the psalms, says "So there is something remarkable here (in this psalm) . . . even in the closing verses also we are aware of just the two figures, the Lord and his treasured one (David), with a background of hostility or danger."[16] In this psalm, it is David who speaks "as sharing the royal task with the true King, God, (and) he could dwell on the thought of his relationship to this supreme sovereign and shepherd."[17] God is the Shepherd of Israel, yet the kings of Israel were called shepherd. In John 21, the Lord Jesus is the Shepherd, yet he charges Peter to share in his role as shepherd. The word feed, together with the shepherd's role of guiding and guarding, is therefore correctly understood in the long tradition of the Church and by scholars to mean true authority, as the king had true authority from God in Israel. What is conferred on Peter is a pastoral authority rooted in Peter's love for Jesus, "Do you love me more than these?" This personal intimacy is also present between David and God in psalm 23. In light of these New Testament foundations, the Petrine trajectory eventually outdistanced the other apostolic trajectories in history after the New Testament period, especially in the West.[18]

---

15. See *Peter in the New Testament*, 145

16. John Eaton, *The Psalms* (London, New York: T& T Clark International, 2003), 122–123.

17. Eaton, *The Psalms*, 123.

18. See *Peter in the New Testament*, 167.

Having established in Chapter I of the decree on the Church that Peter is unique among the apostles in the New Testament, Chapter II goes on to teach that this role does not die with Peter but is permanent in the Church. The Lord who willed the preservation of unity and communion in his Church willed also to insure the continuance of the means to that unity. This chapter concludes with the dogmatic definition that it is "by the institution of the Lord himself... that blessed Peter should have perpetual successors in the primacy over the whole church" and "that the Roman pontiff is... the successor of blessed Peter in this primacy."[19] The bishops were in agreement with the doctrine of these two chapters on the Apostle Peter and with the teaching that the Bishop of Rome is the successor of Peter.

It was Chapter III, enumerating the specific powers of the papal primacy of jurisdiction, which caused extended discussion. The text of the definition is this: "So, then, if anyone says that the Roman Pontiff has merely an office of supervision and guidance, and not the supreme power of jurisdiction over the whole church, and this not only in matters of faith and morals, but also in those which concern the discipline and government of the church dispersed throughout the whole world; or that he has only the principal part, but not the absolute fullness, of this supreme power; or that this power of his is not ordinary and immediate both over all and each of the churches and over all and each of the pastors and faithful: let him be anathema."[20]

In this decree on the Church of Christ, Vatican I unambiguously identifies the Pope as having a primacy of jurisdiction. This means the power of government. "To say... that he (the Pope) has full and supreme power and jurisdiction over the whole Church, not only in matters touching faith and morals, but also over what relates to the discipline and conduct 'of the Church spread throughout the world'... amounts to an assertion of the right and power to rule

19. Tanner, *Decrees of the Ecumenical Councils*, Vol II, 813.

20. Tanner, *Decrees of the Ecumenical Councils*, Vol II, 815.

over the whole Church."[21] This is what the Council teaches about primacy of jurisdiction. It remains to be seen just how this powerful language is to be correctly understood.

The first to speak on this text of the third chapter was Cardinal Joseph Rauscher of Vienna, a leader of the minority. Rauscher, who had been professor of history at Salzburg and had written a two volume history of the Church, had a perspective on history. He began by saying that no one could question that the Pope as Successor of Peter had authority to override or dispense from any provision of church law and that it is self-evident that the Pope could do in any diocese of the world what the bishop of that diocese can do. Still, he objected to calling the universal jurisdiction of the Pope *ordinary* as the proposed text did because, he said, that language could easily open the way to serious misunderstanding. People could easily take it to mean that it is normal for the Pope to govern the affairs of every diocese on a continuing basis.

In answer to this objection, Bishop Zinelli, the official spokesman for the drafting commission, said that the word *ordinary* as it appeared in the text was used in a technical sense and not in its every-day meaning. In canon law, a power is called *ordinary* if it belongs to a particular office and is not a delegated power. For example, it belongs to the ordinary power of the Pope to convoke an ecumenical council. This power belongs to his very office as Pope. Yet he does not convoke a council frequently or on a routine basis. In fact, there have been only three councils in the last four hundred years—Trent, Vatican I and Vatican II. Thus to say that a power is ordinary does not say that it is being used on a continuing basis. Zinelli made it clear that in teaching primacy of jurisdiction, the Church is not teaching a continuing primatial intervention in the world's dioceses as a necessary component of primacy.[22]

---

21. J.M.R.Tillard, *The Bishop of Rome* (London: Society for Promoting Christian Knowledge, 1983), 149.

22. An analysis of this language of the decree is also found in Tillard, *The Bishop of Rome,* 148–149.

Rauscher then raised objection to using the word *immediate.* According to the draft text, the Pope's power of universal jurisdiction is *immediate.* Zinelli explained that this, too, was understood in the meaning of canon law where *immediate* simply means that the Pope does not have to go through someone else or get delegation to exercise this power. It by no means conveys the idea that the Pope is constantly and at all times exercising this immediate authority.

In addition to describing primacy of jurisdiction as *ordinary* and *immediate,* the draft described it as *episcopal.* "This jurisdictional power of the Roman pontiff is both episcopal and immediate."[23] Episcopal authority is the power to teach, govern and sanctify. Here Vatican I enunciates something which was to be more amply elaborated upon in Vatican Council II: Papal primacy of jurisdiction is episcopal precisely because the Pope is a bishop and, by reason of his ordination as a bishop, the Pope is incorporated into and is a member of the College of Bishops. The papal office is embedded in the episcopate and not outside or apart from it. So true is this that the Code of Canon Law of 1983 makes explicit that if someone who is not a bishop is elected Pope, he does not acquire the powers of the papal office at the moment he accepts the election but only later when he is ordained a bishop.[24] When Vatican Council I teaches that the power of the Pope is *episcopal,* it is placing the Pope within the College of Bishops and in an ecclesiology of communion. But the draft also wanted to exclude a mere ceremonial primacy. Thus the power ascribed to the Pope in the universal Church by the word *episcopal* in Vatican Council I is the kind of authority which belongs to a bishop in the pastoral care of his diocese. The bishop's authority is the authority to teach, govern and sanctify. It is not merely a position

23. Tanner, *Decrees of the Ecumenical Councils,* Vol II, 814.

24. *Code of Canon Law* (Washington, DC: Canon Law Society of America, 1998) c. 332.

of honor.[25] The Acts of the Council, together with the explanations of Bishop Zinelli on the floor, make clear that primacy of jurisdiction does mean that the Pope has true authority in the whole Church. This is explicitly stated at the end of the chapter on primacy, where the position according to which "the Roman Pontiff has merely an office of supervision and guidance,"[26] is condemned. But it balances this by the declaration that primacy of jurisdiction does not make the Pope bishop of every diocese: "The power of the supreme pontiff by no means detracts from that ordinary and immediate power of episcopal jurisdiction, by which bishops, who have succeeded to the place of the apostles by appointment of the Holy Spirit, tend and govern individually the particular flocks which have been assigned to them."[27]

Rauscher presented concerns about the strong wording of the text on the grounds that it quarreled with the divine constitution of the Church as mentioned and with the actual history of the Church. But there was another line of thought which was ill at ease with primatial jurisdiction stated in terms which could mean sovereignty and centralization. For at least a hundred and fifty years, there had been dissatisfaction expressed among bishops about Roman centralization. There had also been strong feelings about sovereign centralization among the German episcopate in the eighteenth century over the many things which required dispensations from Rome, as well as the method of the appointment of bishops.[28] While bishops did not want an excess of centralization in Rome, they did want and felt the need of support for the

25. Primacy is not described as the authority of an archbishop because in the Latin Church of the West an archbishop has no true authority in the suffragan sees. But a bishop in his own diocese does have true authority to teach, govern and sanctify.

26. Tanner, *Decrees of the Ecumenical Councils*, Vol II, 814–815.

27. Tanner, *Decrees of the Ecumenical Councils*, Vol II, 814.

28. Klaus Schatz, *Papal Primacy* (Collegeville, MN: Liturgical Press, 1996), 138–143.

episcopate by Rome.[29] Melchers, Archbishop of Cologne, spoke against over-centralization and, in particular, against the limitations placed on bishops, which required them to have frequent recourse to Rome about frequently recurring issues.[30] It was the Croatian Archbishop, Josip Strossmeyer, who spoke the most on the subject, calling for regularly scheduled councils. He insisted that more participative government was rooted in the ecclesial-synodal nature of the Church and not in secular democracy.[31] These bishops, then, saw in sovereignty an injury to the divine constitution of the Church. They saw as well in excessive centralization a wound to the divinely given role of the bishops as successors of the Apostles. It does not do justice to the position of the minority to say that it was an effort to claim power or a move to bring democracy into the Church. Underlying their objections was the divine constitution of the Church.

The true authority of the bishops, then, was explicitly taught in Chapter III. This was still further emphasized by making two additions in the definitive text. These additions came as a result of debate in the Council and show the influence of the minority in shaping the final outcome. First there was the statement just cited: "This power of the supreme pontiff by no means detracts from that ordinary and immediate power of episcopal jurisdiction, by which bishops, who have succeeded to the place of the apostles by appointment of the Holy Spirit, tend and govern individually the flocks which have been assigned to them."[32] Vatican I is saying here that papal primacy is not a diminishment of the role of the bishops and that the episcopate is of divine institution "by appointment of the Holy Spirit." Further, nowhere does the Council teach that

29. Chadwick, *A History of the Popes 1830–1914*, 204.

30. Butler, *The Vatican Council 1869–1870*, 191. Melchers spent six months imprisoned by Bismarck and ten years in exile. Later he renounced his title as cardinal and died as a Jesuit in Rome.

31. Klaus Schatz, *Storia dei concili* (Bologna: Edizione Dehoniane, 1999), 230.

32. Tanner, *Decrees of the Ecumenical Councils*, Vol II, 814.

primacy of jurisdiction is identical with administrative centralization. What Vatican I teaches is the coexistence of two subjects with authority from God—the Pope and the bishops. Both derive their authority from the will of Christ for his Church.[33]

A second statement in the definitive text asserts not only these two divinely appointed authorities—the Pope as Successor of Peter and the bishops as successors of the apostles—but it goes on to assert the correlative truth that it is the Pope's responsibility not to absorb but to reinforce and support the authority of the bishops: "...This power of theirs (i.e. of the bishops) is asserted, supported and defended by the supreme and universal pastor; for St. Gregory the Great says, 'My honour is the honour of the whole Church. My honour is the steadfast strength of my brethren. Then do I receive true honour, when it is denied to none of those to whom honour is due.'"[34] Significantly, these words of St. Gregory come from a letter he addressed to an Eastern bishop, Eulogius of Alexandria, admonishing him not to use excessive language such as referring to the Pope as "universal bishop."[35] Presenting the definitive text for a vote, Zinelli explained that the citation from St. Gregory was added to the decree on primacy precisely to emphasize the truth that papal primacy does not absorb the ordinary and immediate jurisdiction of the bishops. In effect it is a declaration that bishops are not field managers or surrogates of the Pope. Consequently, Vatican I does not declare or teach a sovereign, monarchical primacy. The bishops also have true authority, which, like papal authority, is of divine origin. [36]

---

33. See *The Catechism of the Catholic Church* #877: "It belongs to the sacramental nature of ecclesial ministry that it should have a *collegial character.*"

34. Tanner, *Decrees of the Ecumenical Councils*, Vol II, 814. In antiquity the word *honor* meant not mere external signs of respect, but included the idea of true power and authority. See Brian E. Daley, *Position and Patronage in the Early Church: The Original Meaning of Primacy of Honor*, Journal of Theological Studies (October 1993).

35. Pope Gregory I, *Epistola XXX* (PL 77: 933).

36. Tillard, The Bishop of Rome, 157–164.

A very important factor for understanding this teaching correctly, and a factor too often overlooked, is that in its dogmatic constitution on the catholic faith, Vatican I taught that there is a necessary link which doctrinal truths have among themselves: "Now reason, if it is enlightened by faith, does indeed when it seeks persistently, piously and soberly, achieve by God's gift some understanding... of the mysteries... from the connection of these mysteries with one another..."[37] This necessary connection among dogmatic truths means that a correct understanding of the Petrine office and its prerogatives involves an understanding of the Apostolic office of the bishops and that this fundamental principle—the inherent link among doctrinal truths—is a necessary corrective to the tendency to seize on one doctrinal truth apart from the rest of revealed truth as when the papal office is so exalted as to minimize or trivialize the role of the bishops. Both these offices are revealed truths whose correct understanding requires a grasp of the mutuality of these truths between themselves. To exalt the papal office to the extent that it stands alone, above and apart from the bishops, is a falsification of the teaching of Vatican I. To exalt the office of the bishops so that the Pope is simply an executor of the will of the bishops is also a falsification of the teaching of Vatican I.

The Introduction to the First dogmatic constitution on the church of Christ as enacted by the Council states that the teaching on the primacy "is to be believed and held by all the faithful in accordance with the ancient and unchanging faith of the whole church."[38] The ancient and constant faith of the Church understood the Pope as embedded in the College of Bishops as testified by the whole of the first millennium.[39] The location of the primacy within this testimony of the first millennium is mentioned in the opening

37. *Dogmatic constitution on the catholic faith*, chapter 4. Tanner, *Decrees of the Ecumenical Councils*, Vol II, 808: 30.

38. Tanner, *Decrees of the Ecumenical Councils*, Vol II, 812:10.

39. *Ut unum sint* #55, 56.

sentences of chapter 3 of the Council decree on the primacy.[40] All this weight of evidence makes it clear that Vatican I did not teach a sovereign, monarchical primacy apart from the episcopate or from the rest of the Church. Commenting on this doctrine of Vatican I, Joseph Ratzinger cites with approval the German theologian Heribert Schauf, "...the Church is not like a circle, with a single centre, but like an elipse with two foci, primacy and episcopate."[41]

Pius IX himself is a major witness that Vatican I did not teach a sovereign, monarchical papacy as promoted by the extreme Ultramontanes such as Cappellari, DeMaistre, and by Manning in England. Besides the fact that he approved and promulgated the decrees of the Council, which situated the papacy within the episcopate and as bound by the divine tradition, Pius IX also made two important authoritative statements of his own in which he gave the authentic interpretation of the Council. The first came when he approved the German bishops' declaration on the correct meaning of Vatican I. Joseph Ratzinger says that this statement of the German bishops "provides the key to the full meaning of the Vatican decrees."[42] Their declaration was prompted by a letter sent by the German Chancellor, Bismarck, to German diplomats interpreting primacy of jurisdiction to mean that the Pope had appropriated to himself all the powers of the bishops, thus making himself the sovereign of the Church. The German bishops repudiated this view as false and erroneous, and, in often cited language, said, "We can decisively refute the statement that the bishops have become by reason of the Vatican decrees mere papal functionaries with no personal responsibility."[43] And they added, "According to

---

40. Tanner, *Decrees of the Ecumenical Councils*, Vol II, 813:25. "...supported by the clear witness of holy scripture, and adhering to the manifest and explicit decrees of our predecessors the Roman pontiffs and of general councils..."

41. Karl Rahner, Joseph Ratzinger, *The Episcopate and the Primacy* (New York: Herder and Herder, 1962), 43.

42. Rahner, Ratzinger, *The Episcopate and the Primacy*, 40.

43. Cited by F. Donald Logan in *The Jurist* (21.n.3, July 1961), 291.

the teaching of the Catholic Church the Pope is Bishop of Rome, not bishop of any other city or diocese, not bishop of Cologne or of Breslau."[44] In a letter to the bishops, Pius IX congratulated them, said that theirs was the Catholic interpretation of the Council, and the interpretation of the Holy See, and that the allegations of Bismarck were distorted.[45]

Less than two weeks later, at a consistory for the creation of cardinals, the Pope spoke in solemn language a second time, "... we ratify and in the exercise of the fullness of our apostolic authority we do hereby confirm" the statement of the German bishops.[46]

Because Part II of the Dogmatic Decree on the Church of Christ that included the doctrine on the bishops was never debated or enacted in the Council and some members of the majority continued to maintain that sovereign papal primacy was the norm, Pottmeyer says, "The maximalist interpretation of Vatican I supported Vatican centralization... (and) was persuaded that the dogmas of jurisdictional primacy and papal infallibility were the definitive culmination of ecclesiology, and the ecclesiastical order." [47] And so, while there is overwhelming evidence from the texts and the Acts of the Council, and from the strong words of Pius IX himself, that the doctrinal position of the minority was the accepted teaching, it was virtually ignored in the century following Vatican I and it was this that lay behind the observation that

---

44. Denziger, Shönmetzer, SJ, *Enchridion Symbolorum* 3113; cited by Logan, *Jurist*, 292.

45. Pope Pius IX, *Mirabilis illa Constantia*, March 2, 1875, Denzinger, 3117.

46. Logan, *The Jurist*, 295. This language, "in the fullness of our apostolic authority" has been used by Popes in matters of very grave importance such as the decree of Pius VI in his solemn condemnation of Jansenism and by Paul VI when he promulgated the new form of the sacraments following Vatican Council II. This language of Pius IX therefore indicates that this is a matter of high and weighty importance.

47. Pottmeyer, *Towards a Papacy in Communion*, 111.

"Vatican I has been distorted for over a hundred years"[48]. But why did this happen?[49]

One important reason was that the Acts of the Council were not published for nearly sixty years. Because of this, Part II of the Constitution on the Church, the proposed draft on bishops, was all but unknown. So the actual promulgated text, which was only Part I, focused on the Pope, and, without the Acts, was open to an exaggerated interpretation. But why did it take so long to publish the Acts? It is reasonable to conjecture that since the Council had been abruptly suspended in the fall of 1870 but not formally closed, there was a lingering expectation that the Council would be reconvened, and, when completed, not only the Acts would be published, but a complete dogmatic decree on the church of Christ, including the doctrine on the bishops, would be promulgated. In fact, Pope Pius XI, elected in 1922, gave serious thought to reconvening the Council and even consulted the bishops of the world on the advisability of doing so. [50] He decided against reconvening the Council and formally closed it. It was only when it was clear that the Council would not be reconvened that the Acts were published. If the Acts had been available, including Part II on the bishops, a more balanced understanding of the decrees on primacy and infallibility might have been possible.

A second factor which contributed to an exaggerated interpretation of Vatican I was the very strong language used in the decrees on primacy and infallibility. For instance, the chapter on primacy concludes with these words: "So, then, if anyone says that the Roman pontiff has merely an office of supervision and guidance,

48. Buckley, *Papal Primacy and the Episcopate*, 45.

49. Ratzinger points out that the teaching of Vatican I is much deeper and more complex than many theology text books, particularly the pre-council manuals, would lead us to believe and he says that the teaching of the Vatican I is often oversimplified. Rahner, Ratzinger, *The Episcopate and the Primacy*, 41.

50. When I was Archbishop of Oklahoma City, I discovered a letter of Pope Pius XI in the archives asking my predecessor his opinion on reconvening the Council of 1870.

and not the full and supreme power of jurisdiction over the whole church, and this not only in matters of faith and morals, but also in those which concern the discipline and government of the church dispersed throughout the world; or that he has only the principal part, but not the absolute fullness, of this supreme power; or that this power of his is not ordinary and immediate over all and each of the churches and over all and each of the pastors and faithful: let him be anathema."[51] This powerful language, without benefit of context or explanation, readily leads to the most exaggerated understanding of a sovereign primacy of government. To a great extent, this very strong language was influenced by the history of the nineteenth century which the bishops had experienced. Walter Kasper says, "The Fathers of the First Vatican Council experienced specific historical conditions that led them to formulate things the way they did. The Council majority saw the Church besieged from all sides and in an almost apocalyptic situation. The bishops were traumatized by the Enlightenment, the French Revolution, the absolutism of modern states, by Gallicanism and Episcopalism, and wanted to make sure that the Church would remain capable of action even in extreme situations. This is why they reverted to the modern idea of sovereignty, in such a way that he could act even if he were to be prevented from communicating with the Church. Their statements on primacy were especially conceived for extreme and exceptional situations."[52] And Hermann Pottmeyer pointed out, "The dominant interpretation of the dogma up until Vatican II had not taken this historical factor into account."[53] And he goes on to say, "That interpretation (i.e. the dominant interpretation)

---

51. Tanner, *Decrees of the Ecumenical Councils*, Vol II, 814–815.

52. Walter Kasper, *Introduction to the Theme and Catholic Hermeneutics of the Dogmas of the First Vatican Council* in *The Petrine Ministry*, Cardinal Walter Kasper, ed. (New York, Mahwah, NJ: Newman Press, 2006), 19.

53. Hermann J. Pottmeyer, *Recent Discussions on Primacy in Relation to Vatican I* in Cardinal Walter Kasper, *The Petrine Ministry*, (New York, Mahwah, NJ: Newman Press), 213.

saw the dogma as the result of a logical development of the biblical data and as the perfected formulation of papal primacy."[54] In other words, theology at that time largely confined itself to an analysis of biblical texts without reference to history and regarded the ultramontane understanding of primacy as the final word in ecclesiology. It was this narrow interpretation of the dogma that was taught in the theological manuals used in seminaries all over the world. In fact it is this maximalist interpretation of primacy and infallibility even though it is not the authentic teaching of Vatican I which has prevailed inside the Catholic Church and in public opinion over the period of 150 years.[55]

There is a coherent link between the two Vatican Councils of 1869–70 and 1962–1965[56] and the encyclical letter of Pope John Paul II, *Ut unum sint.* Calling for dialog on new ways of exercising the primacy, Pope John Paul II declared that the papal office must always be exercised "in communion. When the Catholic Church affirms that the office of the Bishop of Rome corresponds to the will of Christ, she does not separate this office from the mission entrusted to the whole body of Bishops... The Bishop of Rome is a member of the 'College', and the Bishops are his brothers in the ministry."[57] Even though the Petrine office has special prerogatives, Pope John Paul repeatedly mentions that the papal office is located within the College of Bishops.[58]

The Encyclical of Pope John Paul II, *Ut unum sint,* therefore develops and applies what was already contained in the texts and in the Acts of Vatican I and Vatican II by placing the Pope within the College of Bishops in a theology of communion, and within the doctrinal and conciliar history of the first millennium. In fact, John Paul explicitly points to the collegial structures of the first

54. Pottmeyer, *Recent Discussions on Primacy in Relation to Vatican I,* 213.

55. Pottmeyer, *Recent Discussions,* pdriscoll@nhdlaw.com, 216.

56. Tanner, *Decrees of the Ecumenical Councils*, Vol II, 862–874.

57. Pope John Paul II, *Ut unum sint* 95.

58. Pope John Paul II, *Ut unum sint,* 94.

millennium as a point of reference to which we must look today.[59] Within this framework it is significant that he never uses the language "primacy of jurisdiction" in the encyclical. He refers to the Pope as Bishop of Rome or as servant of the servants of God. He refers to the Pope's Petrine ministry as "moderator." The Latin word "*moderator*" connotes the idea of keeping things within due limits.[60] Thus Pope John Paul II describes the Church in the first millennium this way, "If disagreements in belief and discipline arose..., the Roman See acted by common consent as moderator."[61] Even so, within this framework he also mentions that without true authority, the papal office is ineffective: "With the power and the authority without which such an office would be illusory, the Bishop of Rome must ensure the communion of all the Churches."[62] Thus while Vatican I had a particular focus on crisis situations, Vatican II and the Encyclical *Ut unum sint* are more focused on how the primacy would be exercised in the Church understood as communion. Correctly understood, then, Vatican Council I and its teaching on primacy is open to an ecclesiology of communion, to a synodal exercise of papal primacy, to the meaningful collegiality of the bishops, and to structures of communion such as the patriarchal and synodal structures which are traditional in the Church.[63]

The majority at Vatican I wanted to exalt the authority of the Pope and reaffirm his powers in as strong a way as possible for the protection and independence of the Church. The bishops were also conscious of the threat to faith from philosophical, scientific and political developments, which was a reason for bolstering as much as possible the teaching authority of the Pope as a means of

59. Pope John Paul II, *Ut unum sint*, 55, 56.

60. Charlton T. Lewis and Charles Short, *A Latin Dictionary* (Oxford, 1962), *moderator*, 1154.

61. Pope John Paul II, *Ut unum sint*, 95.

62. Pope John Paul II, *Ut unum sint*, 94.

63. John R. Quinn, *Ever Ancient, Ever New: Structures of Communion in the Church* (New York/Mahwah, NJ: Paulist Press, 2013), 13–19.

protecting the faith. But the minority saw that the majority, despite its good intentions, was moving in the direction of defining the Pope as an absolute sovereign and monarch. What they saw in this extreme ultramontanism was a break with the divine constitution and tradition of the Church. It was the great achievement of the minority and a sign of its influence that it prevented this erroneous development. It was due to the minority that the primacy was framed in terms of the first millennium and the conciliar tradition, both in the prologue as well as in the chapters of the Constitution on the Church.

To bring this to a conclusion, we can say that in using the expression "primacy of jurisdiction," it was the intention of the Council to ascribe to the Pope the power of authoritative intervention when the needs of the Church required it. The exact circumstances or conditions of such intervention are not determined by the Council, no doubt because all future possible crisis situations could not be clearly foreseen. For example, the bishops of 1870 could not have foreseen the incomparable destructive power which emerged in the twentieth century, including atomic weapons, and the manifold ways the Pope's ability to have contact with the episcopate could be impaired. Even so, the Council did not teach that primacy of jurisdiction made the bishops papal delegates or the Pope the only bishop in the Church. Neither did the Council teach that primacy of jurisdiction means that the only mode of papal primacy is the current structure of highly centralized government which did not exist in the first millennium. When the authentic teaching of Vatican I is correctly understood, it is eminently clear that the teaching of Vatican II on collegiality, and the movement of Pope Francis toward increasing synodality, is rooted in Vatican I and in the ancient conciliar teaching of the Church.

Chapter IV

INFALLIBILITY

Widespread but erroneous understanding of papal infallibility runs from the extreme that the Pope is infallible in almost everything he says and in all his acts, to the other extreme, that the Council teaching was a colossal mistake.[1] It comes as no surprise, then, that at a Vatican Symposium on papal primacy in 1996, one theologian stated, "The way *Pastor Aeternus* has been distorted in its reading has influenced ecclesiology for almost one hundred years."[2] Ian Ker, author of a magisterial biography of Newman, also observes, "The Ultramontanes had not achieved all that they wanted at the Council. But their victory was fairly complete throughout the Church and the repercussions were various."[3] Even the well-known Swiss theologian, Hans Kung, mistakenly believed that it was the maximalist view of infallibility which the Council had defined. Kung's view of Vatican I was rejected by the majority of Catholic theologians.[4] These examples are indications that widespread error about the true meaning of Vatican I has prevailed for a very long time.

1. A recent example of this appears in an on-line comment on a June 22, 2015 piece in *America* (*A Post-Traumatic Church*) by Jeffrey Von Arx. The comment reads: "To be honest, the only thing I ever associate with Vatican I is the doctrine of papal infallibility, arguably the biggest mistake the church has ever made."
2. Buckley, *Papal Primacy and the Episcopate*, 45.
3. Ian Ker, *John Henry Newman* (Oxford, Oxford University Press, 1990), 662.
4. Pottmeyer, *Towards a Papacy in Communion*, 77.

The German theologian, Herrmann Pottmeyer, says, "...the maximalist interpretation of the dogma persists even today. It seems to find confirmation in a phenomenon described as 'sweeping infallibility' or 'galloping infallibility.'"[5] In fact, "One of the main reasons why this dogma is so unpersuasive is the maximalist (erroneous) interpretation that has been given to it. As in the case of the dogma of primacy of jurisdiction, here too it was Catholic catechesis itself that saw to the spread of this maximalist interpretation."[6] The maximalists hoped that by attaching the aura of infallibility to almost everything, greater obedience to Vatican and papal pronouncements would be ensured. But the very opposite is what results—a diminishing of the credibility of the Church and of the Holy See. Exaggeration becomes the mother of alienation. [7]

It is these maximalist distortions, more than the actual doctrine of infallibility, which have contributed to making it an issue of continuing controversy. And it was the distorted view of infallibility which gave rise to the concerns of governments, especially at the time of Vatican I.[8] And it was a distorted view of infallibility which was behind much of the opposition to the election of a Catholic president during the Kennedy campaign.

At the time of the Council, many governments were concerned about the impending definition because they had reason to believe that it would make the *Syllabus* an infallible teaching.[9] In addition, they feared that proclaiming the sovereign primacy of the Pope, together with a maximalist type of infallibility, could mean a revival

5. Pottmeyer, *Towards a Papacy in Communion*, 76–77.

6. Pottmeyer, *Towards a Papacy in Communion*, 76.

7. Pottmeyer, *Towards a Papacy in Communion*, 77.

8. Martina, *Pio IX (1851–1866)*, Vol III, 190.

9. Several factors show that the *Syllabus* could not correctly be understood as an infallible teaching. For one thing, it is merely a collection of propositions taken from a variety of papal talks and documents. Second, there is no hint from the Pope or any other authoritative source that the *Syllabus* carries the note of infallibility. Each of the propositions can be evaluated only by recourse to the original document from which it is taken.

of the doctrine that the Pope is supreme over emperors and kings. They feared that a definition of this kind "could affect the attitude of Catholics to constitutional government; to toleration; to divorce; or to education offered by the State."[10]

In this state of things, the Chancellor of Bavaria, Prince Hohenlohe, proposed that the governments should act together to oppose the infallibility definition, but his idea did not get a positive reaction from some countries. The French political left, with a certain hauteur, took the position that to try to stop the Pope would make it look as if France thought that things he did were important. In England, Gladstone leaned toward some form of intervention because he feared the effect of a definition on Catholics in Ireland, that it might embolden and intensify the negative attitude of Irish Catholics toward the British government. But Lord Clarendon, British Foreign Secretary, was against any government intervention. He counseled Prime Minister Gladstone that it was better to let the Pope do what he wanted because "if the Council declares the pope is infallible, that will only do good because the world will laugh at him."[11] The British envoy in Rome, Odo Russell, was of a similar point of view. He advised that it was better to let the Council follow its course in the belief that a definition of infallibility would weaken the influence of the Catholic Church among the nations.[12] Thus there were fears of possible effects on constitutional states coupled with the hope that a likely negative reaction to the definition would diminish papal authority and subject the Pope to ridicule. Still another reason why some governments felt it was not wise to try to intervene on the issue was that there was popular support among lay Catholics for papal infallibility and they feared a backlash from their citizenry if they appeared to oppose the definition. Ultimately these concerns and fears were founded on the widespread belief that the Council would declare the Pope to be

10. Chadwick, *A History of the Popes 1830–1914*, 192.

11. Chadwick, *A History of the Popes 1830–1914*, 194.

12. Chadwick, *A History of the Popes 1830–1914*, 194.

personally infallible, and infallible in a fairly unlimited range of things, including in particular the *Syllabus*.

Alongside the concerns of the governments, maximalist ideas of infallibility were a cause of controversy inside the Church as well. On one side, the extreme ultramontane wing, including Manning and Ward in England and Ireland, and Pie in France, were reinforcing the fears of governments by vigorously and publicly campaigning for an explicit declaration that the *Syllabus* was infallible teaching, and that infallibility was a personal and almost unlimited attribute of the Pope. On the other side of the issue, there were those like Newman, who opposed the definition for several serious reasons. First, he was concerned about the effect a maximalist definition would have on individual Catholics and the problems of conscience it would cause them. But he also was convinced that the Church needed time to debate the idea. He believed that it was moving too fast on the question of the infallibility of the Pope which had not really been a matter of great theological interest until the nineteenth century. Even though he held it as true, Newman was among a large body of respectable theologians who, prior to the Council, did not regard papal infallibility as a dogma of faith but as a legitimate theological opinion. But he emphatically opposed Manning's maximalist views of an infallibility separate from the episcopate and covering much of the public teaching of the Pope such as encyclicals and the *Syllabus*.

Some French bishops, such as Dupanloup of Orleans, feared that the definition could lead to schisms. Others, such as Döllinger in Germany, were speaking and writing against infallibility as lacking foundation. In distant America, Archbishop Peter Kenrick, a man of considerable scholarship, was among the leaders of opposition to the definition. So there was already an atmosphere of growing controversy as the Council got underway and it was the maximalist idea of infallibility which was foremost in public opinion, as much among those for as those against.

The itinerary from this separate, absolute, omnicompetent papal infallibility of the maximalists to the moderate and balanced doctrine of the actual definition can be traced to the publication in 1820 of the book by Joseph DeMaistre, *The Pope*.[13] The influence of this book on developments leading up to Vatican I cannot be overestimated.[14] The book had two notable effects. It brought the topic of papal authority out of the world of the theologians into the homes of the laity. It was not a theological work and its author was not a theologian. At the same time, the papacy began to be a topic of growing interest and discussion in widely read journals such as *l'Univers* in France and Ward's *Dublin Review*. But the topic also "became enormously explosive even in the political and social order, because according to him (De Maistre), the papacy and papal infallibility were the only guarantees of social order and stability" in a world which, after the French Revolution, the Napoleonic Wars, and the Congress of Vienna, was deeply yearning for renewed stability and something to hold on to.[15] DeMaistre, *l'Univers* and the *Dublin Review* all held up the infallible Pope as the answer to this cry for stability and social order in both church and society.

Thus a long crescendo was building over the years since 1820, when DeMaistre's book first appeared. The crescendo intensified in December 1867, when Pius IX announced his intention to convoke an ecumenical council. It was at this time that Manning and Ignatius von Senestrey, Bishop of Ratisbon, made a vow at the tomb of St. Peter to promote a definition of infallibility vigorously and indefatigably. "From start to finish they stood shoulder to shoulder, straining every nerve to bring about the definition, and in the strongest terms that could be got through the Council..."[16] During the Council, it was primarily Manning and Senestrey "who, at crucial moments, moved heaven and earth to cause pa-

13. Count Joseph De Maistre, *The Pope: Considered In His Relations With The Church, Temporal Sovereignties, Separated Churches, And The Cause Of* Civilization, (London: C. Dolman, tr. Rev. Aeneas McD. Dawson, 1850).

14. Schatz, *Papal Primacy from Its Origins to the Present*, 147–148.

15. Schatz, *Papal Primacy from Its Origins to the Present*, 148.

16. Butler, *The Vatican Council 1869–1870*, 172.

pal infallibility to be defined."[17] During this period, beginning in 1867, as the Council was in preparation, both sides among the bishops formed international committees to discuss and work for or against the definition. By the end of January of 1869, petitions calling for a definition had amassed the signatures of nearly 500 bishops, petitions against the definition got only about 140 signatures. This shows that the bishops of the world were largely in favor of a definition. But a major conflagration erupted in February of 1869, when a provocative article appeared in the influential Jesuit publication *Civiltà Cattolica.* The origins of the article can be traced back to December 9, 1868, a year before the opening of the Council, when the Secretary of State, Cardinal Antonelli, asked the Nuncios in Europe to send periodic reports on public opinion in their countries about the Council. The Nuncio in Paris, Chigi, designated four priests to send him information which he then sent to Rome. One such communique originated with an Abbé Darras, a French historian.[18] Darras claimed that it was the burning desire of lay Catholics that the personal infallibility of the Pope should be proclaimed by acclamation at the Council.[19] This extraordinary proposal, appearing in *Civiltà Cattolica,* widely believed to have been under the direct influence of the Holy See, provoked strong reactions on both sides, justifying the judgement that "A highly crucial factor bringing the topic to the fore was public polarization."[20] A decision was unavoidable. The matter now had to be on the agenda. "Silence on the part of the council would be the equivalent of a negative."[21]

As a result of the tremendous culture shift, both in the world of ideas and in society in general, many were yearning for stability, for

---

17. Schatz, *Papal Primacy from Its Origins to the Present*, 156.

18. Martina judges him a historian of little merit and a convinced intransigent. Martina, *Pio IX (1851–1866)*, Vol III, 155.

19. Martina, *Pio IX (1851–1866)*, Vol III, 154–155.

20. Schatz, *Papal Primacy from Its Origins to the Present*, 155.

21. Schatz, *Papal Primacy from Its Origins to the Present*, 156.

something to hang on to, an anchor. The memory of Pius VII, and the person of Pius IX, both strong figures, provided the answer: the only stabilizing force in the modern world lay in the papacy which remained vigorous and enduring even in the face of extreme adversity. Thus developed the growing focus on the person of the Pope and the increasing reliance on papal teaching. The other current, made up of many bishops who had the experience of constitutional democracies, saw the great benefit of having the Church be free of the pre-Revolution union of Church and State which made possible the interference of kings and rulers in internal church matters. They were convinced that freedom of religion was a great advantage for the Church. They also feared that declaring the Pope to have a personal, wide-ranging infallibility which would include the *Syllabus*, would involve a condemnation of the democratic state, and that it could easily lead to defections from the Church by citizens who could not be brought to believe that freedom of religion was something to be rejected.

But in circles where there was greater theological sophistication, opposition lay also in the fear that the maximalist move to propound an absolute and personal infallibility of the Pope joined with an absolute primacy understood as sovereignty, would in effect be destructive to the divine constitution of the Church, reducing bishops to field managers.

In this atmosphere of conflicting ideas, during the two months from December 1869 through January 1870, the bishops were occupied with electing the various deputations (committees) which would be responsible for the main items to be treated on the agenda of the Council. They also considered a draft of the document on faith but sent it back for revision, and they discussed some other items including a possible catechism, religious orders, and various issues of church discipline and observance. It was only on January 21 that the bishops were given a draft *On the Church of Christ.* It contained nothing about infallibility. But it was sent back for revision because it was too one-sided, dealing mostly with the Pope, to the exclusion of the bishops.

Meanwhile, a considerable number of recommendations had been received from the bishops urging the placement of infallibility on the agenda in the document on the Church. The Council presidents accepted this and, on March 1, the Pope approved the petition of the Council presidents to place infallibility on the agenda. On March 6, this decision, together with a new draft text, was given to the bishops. Until this time, the Pope had maintained a public attitude of neutrality. But his approval of the petition marked his agreement with and support for the ultramontane line.[22]

The comments and recommendations of the bishops on the draft were received by the committee (called officially *The Deputation on Faith)* by March 25. A month later, on April 29, the comments, digested and organized by the theologian consultors, were distributed and, on May 9, the new draft on primacy and infallibility was given to the bishops. The first three chapters, dealing with Peter in the New Testament, with the continuation of the Petrine office in the Bishop of Rome, and with the primacy of the pope, moved along easily, although there was some discussion regarding the primacy of jurisdiction, as explained in the previous chapter, where the issue with the wording of the text which stated that primacy of jurisdiction was ordinary and immediate, gave rise to the fear that it could mean that the Pope took to himself all the authority and powers of the bishops. But when it came to Chapter IV, infallibility was debated at great length and in great detail.

The minority was opposed to a definition of infallibility but not all for the same reasons. Some thought it was not opportune, some thought it had not been sufficiently thrashed out over recent centuries among theologians and needed more time, and some thought it would be harmful to Catholic citizens in modern democratic states. But even among the majority who favored the definition, there were those who held that the Pope could define only doctrines found in the deposit of faith, in divine revelation, and that infallibility of dogmatic definitions was due not to a divine inspiration

---

22. Martina, *Pio IX (1851–1866)*, Vol III, 185.

given the Pope, but to the Providence of God watching over the Church and preventing error. But among the majority some, including leaders like Manning, did hold and vigorously promoted extreme views, including the idea that the Pope's infallibility was an almost oracular power and that it extended to any kind of solemn pronouncement such as encyclicals, the canonization of saints, the approval of religious orders, and, of course, the *Syllabus.* Thus neither the minority nor the majority was characterized by a single point of view. There were shades of difference within each group.

On May 13, Pie, spokesman for the Deputation on Faith, gave the official report on the new draft. He made very precise distinctions. When he spoke of infallibility, he stated that the Pope is the voice of the Church but not because he receives his power from the Church.[23] Rather, he can never define a dogma unless he has certitude that it is contained in revelation and also that it is held by the whole Church. The Pope therefore is always united with the Church in his dogmatic definitions and cannot be separated from the rest of the Church. This statement of the issue, which limited the scope of infallibility, found a positive response among the minority, but some of the majority who still wanted a doctrine of personal and separate infallibility defined.[24]

A speech by the Dominican Cardinal Guidi was a major turning point in the debate on infallibility; Butler calls it "one of the sensations of the Council."[25] Guidi, a Dominican, had been a professor of theology and was respected for his learning. Though he was in favor of a definition, he, like some others in the majority, had concerns about any definition which would be framed in terms of separate and personal infallibility of the Pope. On June 18, 1870, addressing the issue of personal infallibility, and basing his position on the fourteenth century Dominican, Antoninus of Florence, Guidi proposed that the decree should speak of the infallibility of the papal

---

23. This means that the Pope is not merely the delegate of the bishops.

24. Martina, *Pio IX (1851–1866),* Vol III, 201.

25. Butler, *The Vatican Council 1869–1870*, 353.

magisterium and not of the personal infallibility of the Pope, and he thus proposed that the title of chapter IV should be changed from "The Infallibility of the Roman Pontiff" to "the infallibility of his dogmatic definitions."[26] Then, addressing the position that the Pope was outside and above the Church, separate in making dogmatic definitions, he went on to propose that the decree should make clear that the Pope is bound to use ordinary human diligence in deciding to make a dogmatic definition, diligence embodied in such things as prayer, consultation and study of the issue. He went on to say that a normal means for the Pope to arrive at a decision was consultation with the bishops, who are the witnesses of the faith of their churches.[27]While there was a positive reaction to Guidi's proposals even among the majority, there were still those who continued to hold out for a personal and separate infallibility. The drafting committee, (Deputation on Faith) outright rejected Guidi's views as Gallican.[28] But the controversy over Guidi's proposals gradually subsided, and despite the previous criticism, Guidi had a positive influence on the final wording of the decree. Thus the title of chapter IV when promulgated was in fact changed from "The Infallibility of the Roman Pontiff" to "The Infallible Magisterium of the Roman Pontiff." And in the text of the chapter itself, an extensive section was added concerning the historical fact of Popes consulting with the bishops and with the wider Church. The text reads, "The Roman pontiffs, too, as the circumstances of the time or the state of affairs suggested, sometimes by summoning ecumenical councils or consulting the opinion of the churches scattered throughout the world, sometimes by special synods, sometimes by taking advantage of other useful means afforded by divine providence, defined as doctrines to be held those things which, by God's help, they knew to be in keeping with sacred scripture and the apostolic traditions."[29]

---

26. Butler, *The Vatican Council 1869–1870*, 353.

27. Butler, *The Vatican Council 1869–1870*, 354.

28. Martina, *Pio IX (1851–1866)*, Vol III, 207.

29. Tanner, *Decrees of the Ecumenical Councils*, Vol II, 815–816.

This portion of the Council chapter on infallibility mentions councils and synods—collegial structures—and "consulting the opinion of the churches scattered throughout the world" which Pius IX did in fact do prior to the dogmatic definition of the Immaculate Conception. Guidi, initially strongly rebuffed, lived to see some positive results of his proposals.

However, the minority continued to hope and work for the placement in the definition itself of wording that would state that the Pope, in making dogmatic definitions, does so based on the witness of the bishops or by some consultation with the bishops. But there was steadfast resistance to placing any juridical conditions on the Pope. The reason was that after the experiences of Jansenism and Gallicanism and the serious problems of the French Revolution and Napoleon in the 18th and 19th century, there was a general conviction that the Pope had to be able to act decisively and quickly to prevent confusion and widespread dissemination of doctrinal error in a crisis situation. The reasoning was that if conditions were made part of the definition itself, there would be endless controversy over whether they had been fulfilled, leaving an open field for the growth and propagation of ambiguity and doctrinal error.[30]

The question, then, that most deeply divided the bishops on papal infallibility was the question of whether the consultation and consent of the episcopate was a juridical condition on which infallibility of dogmatic definitions would depend. The committee on faith (Deputation on Faith) adamantly refused to allow such a condition to be placed in the actual formula of the definition itself and most of the majority agreed with this. On July 13, five days before the final solemn vote, the bishops had a preliminary vote on the draft. In a last minute effort to accommodate the concerns of the minority, the revised text of the chapter included a lengthy section describing how the Popes over the course of history had in fact consulted the bishops in a variety of ways. The implication was that since this is the usual course the Pope has followed over the

30. Schatz, *Papal Primacy from Its Origins to the Present*, 161.

centuries, it could be assumed that he would likely do the same in the future. But this was not stated explicitly in the formula of the definition. The majority of the bishops voted for the draft. But a significant minority, between a quarter and a third of those present in Rome, did not want the text without explicit mention of the consent of the episcopate. Some absented themselves from this session, including Cardinal Antonelli, Secretary of State. Eighty-eight voted against and sixty-two voted for the draft with reservations. But the large number voting against, especially after the additions made to the text of July 13, shocked the majority and greatly disturbed the Pope, reinforcing his conviction that all efforts to conciliate with the minority were useless. The Pope conveyed his position to the Committee on Faith on June 14 and, in light of this, the final sentence of the chapter was expanded to read "Therefore, such definitions of the Roman pontiff are of themselves, and not by the consent of the church, irreformable."[31] On July 16, a vote was taken on the insertion of this new language into the text of the definition and it won by a large majority. At the final solemn vote two days later, *Pastor aeternus* passed with 535 votes. These are the words of the actual dogmatic definition: "*. . . we teach and define as a divinely revealed dogma that when the Roman Pontiff speaks ex cathedra, that is, when, in the exercise of his office as shepherd and teacher of all Christians, in virtue of his supreme apostolic authority, he defines a doctrine concerning faith or morals to be held by the whole church, he possesses, by the divine assistance promised to him in blessed Peter, that infallibility which the divine Redeemer willed his church to enjoy in defining doctrine concerning faith or morals. Therefore, such definitions of the Roman pontiff are of themselves, and not by the consent of the church, irreformable.*"[32]

31. Tanner, *Decrees of the Ecumenical Councils*, Vol II, 816. See Klaus Schatz *Storia dei Concili* (Bologna: Edizioni Dehoniane, 1999), 244. Schatz here says that the Pope ordered the insertion of the phrase "and not by the consent of the church."

32. Tanner, *Decrees of the Ecumenical Councils*, Vol II, 816.

This decree lays down four conditions, all of which must be met if a doctrinal pronouncement is to be held as infallible. First, the Pope must intend to exercise his supreme apostolic authority as shepherd and teacher of all Christians. Second, he must define the doctrine. Third, the doctrine must be a doctrine concerning faith or morals. And, fourth, the Pope must intend that this doctrine be held by the whole Church. The first condition means that while he can speak as a private theologian, or as Bishop of Rome, his teaching is infallible only when he is speaking as head of the universal Church and as shepherd and teacher of all Christians and in virtue of his supreme apostolic authority. The word *define* here means "to give a definitive judgment which puts an end to freedom of opinion on a question and decisively establishes some truth as an element of the normative faith" of the Church.[33] The doctrine is restricted to a doctrine of faith or morals. "Now only a truth which has been revealed to us by God 'for the sake of our salvation' can be defined as a dogma of faith. In other words, the object of solemn definition as dogma has to be a 'doctrine of faith or morals' which is in itself formally contained in the 'deposit of revelation.'"[34] For example, the appropriateness and usefulness of the Pope retaining the temporal power of the Papal States is an administrative question having nothing to do with divine revelation. Therefore it could not be an object of an infallible definition.[35] Finally, the Pope must intend that this doctrine be held by the whole Church. These four things taken together are what the words *ex cathedra* mean.

The decree says that a defined doctrine is "to be held." This is very precise language used for a very precise purpose. If the text had said "to be believed," it would have restricted infallible teaching only to those things which are divinely revealed. But the text

---

33. Francis A. Sullivan S.J., *Magisterium* (Dublin: Gill and Macmillan, Goldenbridge, 1983), 102.

34. Sullivan, *Magisterium*, 102.

35. Proposition #76 of the *Syllabus* condemned support for the abrogation of the Papal States. D 2976.

means to assert that the Church can also define truths which, though not revealed, are necessarily connected with revealed truth. An example of this kind of truth would be the validity of the election of the Pope, or of an ecumenical council. If the Church could not have certainty about the valid election of the Pope or about the legitimacy of an ecumenical council, it would follow that it could not have certainty about the teaching of that Pope or that Council. So the text means to include both divinely revealed truths as well as truths, not revealed, which have a necessary connection with what is divinely revealed.

Analysis of the dogmatic decree of Vatican I shows that the widespread and erroneous understanding of papal infallibility as extending to almost everything and as a personal attribute (*separate, personal and absolute)* of the Pope, was not the doctrine defined by *Pastor aeternus.*[36] The charism of infallibility does not come into play in every exercise of papal or conciliar teaching as the maximalists wanted.[37] Certainly this means that the *Syllabus* is not infallible teaching. The four conditions contained in the dogmatic decree show that dogmatic definitions are a rare occurrence and that most papal teaching is not a dogmatic definition.

The maximalist party also wanted and worked for a decree which would explain infallibility as the personal attribute of the Pope. But the decree shows that infallibility belongs to the teaching itself. The Pope, speaking *ex cathedra,* in that act is accompanied by the divine assistance which makes that teaching immune from error. In the text we read, "he possesses, by the divine assistance promised to him in blessed Peter, that infallibility which the divine Redeemer willed his church to enjoy…"[38] The second proof that the Council did not teach infallibility as personal attribute of the Pope is that the title of Chapter IV was changed from "The Infal-

36. One of the best accounts of infallibility is found in Sullivan, *Magisterium*, 79–118.

37. Sullivan, *Magisterium*, 99.

38. Tanner, *Decrees of the Ecumenical Councils*, Vol II, 816.

libility of the Roman Pontiff" to the title which the Council voted, "On the Infallible Teaching Authority of the Roman Pontiff." The title of the chapter was purposely changed to make clear that infallibility of teaching is due not to a personal, inherent attribute of the Pope as an individual, but rather as an attribute to the Pope only in the supreme exercise of his teaching authority, which receives the divine assistance that renders the teaching immune from error.

The widespread erroneous belief also holds that the Pope is separate from the episcopate and the Church in making infallible definitions. The paragraph containing the doctrinal decree explicitly recalls the tradition of the Church, "Therefore, faithfully adhering to the tradition received from the beginning of the Christian faith . . ."[39] That tradition shows the Roman Pontiff as embedded in the Church and in the episcopate. When he speaks "as shepherd and teacher of all Christians, in virtue of his supreme apostolic authority," he is speaking not as a private person or a private theologian. Therefore he is not separate from the episcopate.

A third point which has been distorted are the words ". . . *such definitions of the Roman Pontiff are of themselves, and not by the consent of the church, irreformable."* These words were added at the express direction of Pius IX. Father Francis Sullivan says this: "It is historically certain that what the majority of Vatican I intended by the phrase was the definitive repudiation of the fourth of the Articles of the Gallican Clergy of 1682, which was that a doctrinal decision made by the pope would be irreformable only if it obtained the consent of the Church. There is no doubt about the fact that the 'Church' in this Article really means 'the episcopate.' The precise target at which Vatican I aimed was the idea of such a juridical dependence of papal definitions on episcopal approval that there could be a legitimate appeal from a papal definition to the judgment of the rest of the episcopal college, which could conceivably reverse the Pope's decision. To admit such juridical dependence of papal definitions on episcopal approval would amount to denying

39. Tanner, *Decrees of the Ecumenical Councils*, Vol II, 816.

primacy and infallibility to papal magisterium and attributing it uniquely to the magisterium of the whole episcopate."[40] Thus, the clause "of themselves and not by the consent of the Church" is intended to rule out juridical dependence of papal definitions on episcopal consent. But Sullivan goes on to point out that "it does not, and indeed cannot rule out a real dependence of papal definitions on the faith of the Church. For the Pope can define as a dogma of faith only what is contained in the deposit of revelation."[41] And he adds, "The Pope has no source of revelation that is independent of the faith-life of the Church."[42] If the dogmatic definition included a juridical requirement of approval or consultation with the episcopate, in a crisis situation where such approval or consultation could not be obtained, the Church would be paralyzed. In the modern world such a crisis situation might conceivably be created by an atomic attack or some other disaster which would prevent communication of the Pope with the episcopate, as happened when Pius VII was held incommunicado by Napoleon.

An important and authoritative factor which enabled the majority at the Council to vote for the final text was the clarifying speech given on July 11, 1870, by the official spokesman for the drafting committee, the Austrian Bishop Vincent Gasser. He has been called "the most prominent theologian of the Council."[43] His speech was very thorough covering all aspects of the topic of infallibility and lasted nearly four hours. It is regarded by some scholars as the best account of the controversy over infallibility.[44] The

40. Sullivan, *Magisterium*, 103.

41. Sullivan, *Magisterium*, 103.

42. Sullivan, *Magisterium*, 104.

43. Butler, *The Vatican Council 1869–1870*, 386.

44. The full text of this speech is found in the Acts of the Council recorded in G.D. Mansi, *Collectio conciliorum recentiorum*, ed. J.B. Martin and L. Petit (Arnheim and Leipzig, 1923–27), Vol IV, 1204. An English translation of this speech with commentary and notes may be found in James T. O'Connor, *The Gift of Infallibility* (Boston: St. Paul Editions, 1986; San Francisco: Ignatius Press, 2008).

Gasser address is in fact "the key to the proper interpretation of chapter four of *Pastor aeternus* (the chapter on infallibility) since the bishops voted on it as explained by Gasser representing the Deputation *de fide*."[45]

After pointing out that primacy is based on the truth that the Pope is the successor of Peter, which was explained at the beginning of Chapter IV, he makes the point that primacy includes the supreme power of teaching and that therefore infallibility is a function of primacy. He then goes on to respond to the chief objections raised against the definition.

The first is that infallibility would alter the divine constitution of the Church and make councils unnecessary. To this Gasser replied "they will be necessary in the future as they were necessary in the past."[46] Councils are not necessary, Gasser explained, in order to know the truth because the faithful of Christ can know the truth through the ordinary magisterium of the bishops in communion with the Apostolic See. But councils are necessary at times in order to repress errors and in those cases "the most solemn judgment of the Church in matters of faith and morals is, and always will be, the judgment of an ecumenical council in which the Pope passes judgment together with the bishops of the Catholic world who meet and judge together with him."[47] Thus Gasser made it clear that the definition of infallibility did not, in fact, make councils superfluous.

Next Gasser took up the second objection: if the Pope is infallible, councils cannot really be free because the Pope alone will be the real judge of truth. Gasser rejected this saying that if there has been no dogmatic definition by the Pope, then in fact the Pope is leaving the matter to be dealt with by the Council.[48]

In dealing with the next objection, Gasser touched on three words which had been at the root of nearly all the controversy

---

45. O'Connor, *The Gift of Infallibility*, 3.

46. O'Connor, *The Gift of Infallibility*, 37.

47. O'Connor, *The Gift of Infallibility*, 38.

48. O'Connor, *The Gift of Infallibility*, 38–40.

surrounding infallibility: personal, separate, absolute. With meticulous precision, he began by saying that, yes, infallibility is personal. "Therefore, having rejected the distinction between the Roman Church and the Roman Pontiff, between the See and the possessor of the See, that is, between the universal series and the individual Roman Pontiffs succeeding each other in this series, we defend the personal infallibility of the Roman Pontiff inasmuch as this prerogative belongs, by the promise of Christ, to each and every legitimate successor of Peter in his chair."[49]

But it is not personal if that means that it belongs to the Pope as a private individual. "...it (infallibility) does not belong to the Roman Pontiff inasmuch as he is a private person...but as the person of the Roman Pontiff or a public person, that is, as head of the Church in his relation to the Church Universal...But the divine assistance promised to him, by which he cannot err, he only enjoys as such when he really and actually exercises his duty as supreme judge and universal teacher of the Church in disputes about the Faith....the Pope is only infallible when by a solemn judgment, he defines a matter of faith or morals for the Church universal."[50]

Taking up the next objection he was again extremely precise and affirmed that papal infallibility is indeed *separate* in the sense that it is founded on the special promise of Christ to Peter and on the assistance of the Holy Spirit. It can be called separate in the sense that no other individual bishop can teach definitively or definitively bind the universal Church. Gasser says, "It is able to be called separate, or rather distinct because it rests on a special promise of Christ and therefore on a special assistance of the Holy Spirit, which assistance is not one and the same with that which the whole body of the teaching Church enjoys when united with its head. For since Peter and his successor are the center of ecclesiastical unity, whose task it is to preserve the Church in a unity of faith and charity and to repair the Church when disturbed, his condition

49. O'Connor, *The Gift of Infallibility*, 41.

50. O'Connor, *The Gift of Infallibility*, 41–42.

and his relation to the Church are completely special; and to this special and distinct condition corresponds a special and distinct privilege."[51] But Gasser goes on to explain that infallibility, though separate in the sense explained, does not exclude the cooperation of the Church and, in particular, of the bishops, because "the infallibility of the Roman Pontiff does not come to him in the manner of inspiration or of revelation but through a divine assistance." And he makes the important conclusion "Therefore the Pope, by reason of his office and the gravity of the matter, is held to use the means suitable for properly discerning and aptly enunciating the truth." [52]

To summarize this complex account, it is clear that the majority of the bishops at the Council wanted the definition of infallibility. By and large the Catholic people also wanted it. It is therefore a distortion to say that the definition was enacted because the Pope railroaded it through a resistant Council. The Pope personally wanted the definition and he personally favored and worked hard for the more extreme ideas of Manning and Senestrey. But these extreme ideas did not prevail in the final decree. That the Pope's personal views did not prevail is a sign that the Council felt free and did not believe it was being forced into a certain position by the Pope. On July 18, 1870, in the solemn session, the four chapters of the decree *Pastor aeternus*, which included the chapter on infallibility, were passed with 535 votes for and only two against.[53]

Pius IX himself authenticated the moderate interpretation of the Council teaching. In 1871, Joseph Fessler, Bishop of St. Pölten in Austria, published a book entitled *The True and the False Infallibility of the Popes.*[54] Fessler was well read in the Fathers of the Church,

51. O'Connor, *The Gift of Infallibility*, 42–43.

52. O'Connor, *The Gift of Infallibility*, 43. See also the analysis of Tillard, *The Bishop of Rome*, 172–178.

53. Martina, *Pio IX (1851–1866)*, Vol III, 215.

54. Joseph Fessler, *The True and the False Infallibility of the Popes* (San Bernardino, CA: St. Pius X Press, 2016). This is a reprint of the original third edition, translated by Ambrose St. John of the Birmingham Oratory in 1875.

in history, and in canon law. Because of these qualities, Pius IX appointed him to be General Secretary of the Vatican Council. He was well informed and he had the confidence of the Pope. Fessler wrote that "the reasons given for the definition and the historical account of the doctrine (in the decree) are of immense importance for a right understanding of the matter."[55] And he states that the historical examples of papal teaching given in the text are to be understood as an indication of how solemn papal teaching will be done in the future.[56] The Pope's teaching, he says, is infallible only under the conditions mentioned in the decree, that is, when that teaching was given *ex cathedra* as explained above. In concise language he explains that the Pope has the gift of infallibility "only as supreme teacher of truths necessary for salvation revealed by God, not as supreme priest, not as supreme legislator in matters of discipline, not as supreme judge in ecclesiastical questions, not in respect of any other questions over which his highest governing power in the Church may otherwise extend."[57] Pottmeyer says that the debate in the Council served to make clear that divine assistance in papal teaching and cooperation or consultation with the bishops are not in competition with each other but that, on the contrary, "God's assistance (to the Pope) includes an appropriate participation of the bishops..."[58]

Pius IX wrote a letter to Fessler praising his book. The Pope's praise was not perfunctory, based on a report prepared by his staff. On the contrary, the Pope had the book translated into Italian and read it himself. This was proof that Pius IX gave an informed endorsement to a moderate view of infallibility which included the bishops as witnesses of faith. Fessler's book, so clearly endorsed by the Pope, held that the infallible teaching office of the Pope was not separate from the Church and that the Council decree, properly

55. Fessler, *The True and the False Infallibility of the Popes*, 37.

56. Fessler, *The True and the False Infallibility of the Popes*, 41.

57. Fessler, *The True and the False Infallibility of the Popes*, 43.

58. Pottmeyer, *Towards a Papacy in Communion*, 108.

understood, meant the Pope's infallible teaching had to be rooted in the sources of faith, the Scripture and divine tradition.[59] Fessler was thus particularly convincing to wavering elements of the minority because he had been General Secretary of the Council and had voted with the majority. And so it was this book, together with the substantial praise it received from Pius IX, that enabled many bishops of the minority to accept the Council decree in good faith. They were reassured that the authentic teaching of the Council was not a sovereign papal authority outside and above the episcopate and the Church, and that the teaching was clearly in line with the patristic and conciliar teaching of the past. [60] Papal approbation of both Fessler's work and of the statement of the German bishops are in reality an official and authoritative interpretation of the meaning of Vatican I by Pius IX himself.[61]

Until the 19th century, the infallible teaching magisterium of the Pope was not an issue of serious controversy nor was it a focus of special interest, even though some earlier theologians had made reference to it.[62] Given the relative newness of the idea and the absence of controversy, just what was it that moved the Council to develop this dogmatic decree? For one thing, it was the environment of the 19th century. Given the inability of the episcopate in France to save the Church and the stunning intervention of Pius VII at the time, there was a growing sense that, in time of real upheaval and confusion, the Pope was the one person who could consolidate the Church. At very critical moments, decisions have to be made and delay only serves to exacerbate the harm. The bishops thus were convinced of the need for speed in some possible situations and

59. Martina, *Pio IX (1851–1866)*, Vol III, 228.

60. Pottmeyer, *Towards a Papacy in Communion*, 109.

61. Martina, *Pio IX (1851–1866)*, Vol III, 228.

62. See St. Thomas Aquinas, *Summa Theologiae* II–II, q. 1, a 10, resp. Thomas here says that it belongs to the Supreme Pontiff to determine authoritatively matters of faith so that all can believe them with unshakable faith (*sententialiter determinare ea quae sunt fidei, ut ab omnibus inconcussa fide teneantur*).

for an authoritative voice. At the same time, the very conditions with which the text of Chapter IV surrounds the definition imply that this power is not one which would be frequently used: it must be *ex cathedra*, that is, it must be in virtue of his supreme office as shepherd and teacher of all Christians, about "a doctrine concerning faith or morals to be held by the whole Church"[63] and it must be done as definitive. It is not an everyday or ordinary way of papal teaching. This is one reason why main-line theologians state that it is particularly meant for crisis situations.[64] But the Pope, even when he speaks in a crisis situation, cannot be and is not separated from his union with the Church and the bishops. The Pope is in the Church, he is a member of the Church, and as a bishop, he is permanently located within the body or college of the bishops, serving as its head.

It is clear, then, that the actual teaching of Vatican I does not support the extreme position of those mentioned at the beginning of this chapter who maintain that the Pope is "infallible in almost everything he says and in all his acts." The position of the maximalists was that infallibility of the Pope was separate and absolute. It is clear that the actual teaching of the decree *Pastor aeternus* in its fourth chapter rejected both these claims. It rejected papal teaching authority as "separate" by explicitly setting out the historical practice of the papacy and by locating that teaching office within the Church. The "Church" as used here is meant to indicate the bishops. That papal teaching authority is not absolute and is limited to the papal infallible teaching office to "faith and morals" and by the conditions named in the definition.

But what of the other extreme that "the Council teaching was a colossal mistake"? One major reason behind the call to nullify Vatican I is precisely the erroneous belief that it taught the maximalist idea that the Pope is in fact infallible in a wide range of areas. In reality, it has been shown that the Council did not teach

63. Tanner, *Decrees of the Ecumenical Councils*, Vol II, 816.

64. Buckley, *Papal Primacy and the Episcopate*, 62–74.

the maximalist idea of infallibility. Hence the basis for the call to repudiate the infallibility doctrine—that the Pope is infallible in almost everything—does-not exist.

Newman gives a persuasive line of reasoning in support of an infallible teaching office in the Church.[65] He first affirms that the basic principle of the doctrine of infallibility in *Pastor Aeternus* is that "the Pope has that same infallibility which the Church has." But he goes on to say that if we ask what is the nature of the Church's infallibility then we must address the further issue of what the nature of Christianity is as a revealed religion. In pursuing this further, he asserts that Christ "willed the Gospel to be a revelation" public, fixed and permanent, and accordingly he created a structure, a society of human beings, to be its home, its instrument and its guarantee.[66] He gave the Apostles and their successors their great commission and charged them to teach their converts all over the earth to observe "all things whatever He had commanded them," and then He added, "Lo, I am with you always, even to the end of the world" (Matt 28:20).The commission to which Newman refers here is the commission to teach all over the world, to teach all things which they have received from the Lord Jesus, and to teach under the certainty that "I am with you always to the end of the world." The promise of supernatural help did not end with the Apostles personally, in light of the fact that the Lord Jesus promised to be with them to the consummation of the world, implying that they would have successors and that he would be with the successors as he had been with them. Newman sums it up, "For, if the Church, initiated in the Apostles and continued in their successors, has been set up for the direct object of protecting, preserving, and declaring the Revelation, and that, by means of the guardianship and providence of its Divine Author, we are led on to perceive that, in asserting this, we are in other words asserting that, so far as the

65. See John Henry Newman, *Duke of Norfolk* in *Difficulties of Anglicans*, Vol. II, 320.

66. Newman, *Duke of Norfolk* in *Difficulties of Anglicans*, 322.

message entrusted to it is concerned, the Church is infallible; for what is meant by infallibility in teaching but that the teacher in his teaching is secured from error? And how can fallible man be thus secured except by a supernatural infallible guidance?" He concludes, "Such then being, in its simple outline, the infallibility of the Church, such too will be the Pope's infallibility, as the Vatican Fathers have defined it."[67]

He asserts that inasmuch as Christ gave a divinely revealed truth to His Church, He would most certainly have made provision for preserving that truth. Newman goes on to point out that a book—the Bible—cannot in and of itself preserve the truth since every written text requires interpretation. He further points out that a State Church cannot and in fact does not preserve revealed truth as history itself shows. Therefore there is need of a living voice which can set limits, raise challenges, and declare with authority what the revealed truth is and what it means.

---

67. Newman, *Duke of Norfolk* in *Difficulties of Anglicans*, 323.

Chapter V

WAS VATICAN I INVALID?

In Chapters III and IV, we saw the manifold concerns of bishops in the matter of primacy and infallibility and how the extensive debates led to refinements and clarifications which produced a teaching on both topics which was moderate and surrounded by clearly stated conditions. Primacy was not taught in a way which meant that the Pope was constantly determining every detail of church life in every diocese, or that by reason of primacy, the Pope was the only bishop and the other bishops were his surrogates or legates. Similarly, infallibility was not taught as a personal attribute of the Pope, but as an aspect of divine providence over the Church which prevented dogmatic definitions from error.

However, in 1981, the Swiss theologian, August Hasler, published a book in which he contends that Vatican I was not a valid council.[1] He gives four reasons to argue against the validity of the council. First, he places great emphasis on the contention that the Pope was mentally incompetent making it impossible for him to understand or make decisions in a responsible way.[2] A second reason is that the Pope exerted inordinate pressure on the minority bishops during the council and, as a result, the council was not free.[3] Then, be-

1. August Bernhard Hasler, *How the Pope Became Infallible*, (Garden City, NY: Doubleday & Company, Inc., 1981).
2. Hasler, *How the Pope Became Infallible*, 124–128. See also Martina, *Pio IX (1851–1866)*, Vol III, 114.
3. Hasler, *How the Pope Became Infallible*, 141–145.

cause some 120 bishops did not participate in the final solemn vote, the decrees are invalid because there was not moral unanimity.[4] Finally, even though almost all the minority bishops did accept the decrees after the council, Hasler contends that this acceptance was only external compliance and not a sincere acceptance of the decrees.[5] In what follows, I will examine these four objections.

Hasler has been the chief proponent of the claim that Pius IX was not competent to make responsible decisions, particularly those having to do with the council.[6] In support of this claim, he points to the fact that the Pope was an epileptic, even though there is no evidence that he ever suffered a seizure after his ordination as a priest on April 10, 1819.[7] Hans Kung, in his introduction to Hasler's work, goes so far as to say that Pius IX was "mentally disturbed,"[8] although he does not give any source for this claim. There are, however, many things which show Pius IX was clearly in possession of his mental powers and a man of basic equilibrium.

To begin with, there are many reports that the Pope was a very affable, friendly person, with great personal charm and a great sense of humor. Speaking about the personality of the Pope, Owen Chadwick makes the observation that the unprecedented influence Pius IX had on the growth and direction of the Church was no doubt due to his long papacy of thirty-two years, but "it was also due to his unusual personality. He was outgoing and unpompous. Everyone who met him, except on the rare occasions when he was angry, agreed to his charm and friendliness... He easily made friends. Nothing about him was remote, or shut away."[9]

---

4. Hasler, *How the Pope Became Infallible*, 69.
5. Hasler, *How the Pope Became Infallible*, 221–226.
6. Hasler, *How the Pope Became Infallible*, 105–107.
7. Martina, *Pio IX (1851–1866)*, Vol III, 171, n.139. Petit mal epilepsy occurs most often in patients under the age of 20 and usually in children age 6–12.
8. Hasler, *How the Pope Became* Infallible, 17.
9. Chadwick, *The Popes and European Revolution*, 112–113.

The Cambridge professor, Eamon Duffy, describes Pius IX as "almost as attractive as Pope John XXIII—devout, kindly if emotionally volatile, unstuffy, at ease in the company of women...he loved to meet people, he had a boisterous but unmalicious sense of humour, he took clouds of snuff."[10]

Gladstone spent nearly an hour with Pius IX on October 22, 1866, three years before the opening of the council. In his report to the government he makes no reference to any mental deficiency, but underlines the openness and cordiality of the Pope.[11] On December 18, 1869, ten days after the opening of the council, the representative of Great Britain in Rome, Odo Russell, reported to London, "The Pope is as cheerful and happy and calm as possible. He is benevolent, paternal and jocular with his opponents and won't allow a word to be said against them in his presence...The independent Bishops have gone to him in fear and trembling...and have come away...charmed by his wit and humour."[12] Emile Ollivier, Premier of France at the time of the Vatican Council, wrote two volumes on the Council.[13] He devotes three pages to praising Pius IX, noting his personal charm and sense of humor.[14] Ollivier never makes any mention of signs of mental incompetence. Two things enhance the credibility of Ollivier's account: he was regarded as a careful and excellent historian[15] and he did not evaluate Pius IX from the vantage point of a Catholic, since he was not a member of the Church. There are

---

10. Eamon Duffy, *It Takes All Sorts To Make A Saint,* (The Tablet, September 9, 2000).
11. Martina, *Pio IX (1851–1866),* Vol III, 6.
12. Martina, *Pio IX (1851–1866),* Vol III, 172, n.139.
13. Emile Ollivier, *L'Eglise Et L'Etat Au Concile Du Vatican* (*Triosieme Edition*), (Paris, Garnier Freres, 1877).
14. Ollivier, *L'Eglise Et L'Etat Au Concile Du Vatican* (*tome second*), 43–46.
15. Butler, *The Vatican Council 1869–1870,* 80: "This book being, in certain aspects of the external history, the most important work on the Council...I have to say that of all books of history I have read, this one comes perhaps the nearest to the ideal of historical objectivity and impartiality."

thus substantial witnesses against the claim of mental incompetence on the part of the Pope.

Even the most balanced human being can have moments of anger and lose his temper. Eamon Duffy points out, "It was Pio Nono's misfortune to be Pope during a period of unprecedented political and intellectual turmoil. Possibly no Pope since Gregory the Great has faced so daunting a set of challenges."[16] Living with overwhelming responsibilities and under tremendous pressure, especially in the final month of the council, it is understandable that the Pope sometimes slipped into displays of anger and said things impulsively. A famous incident, often used to portray Pius as an unbalanced megalomaniac is the story of his shouting "I am the tradition." Owen Chadwick says that this is the most famous incident of the council period, "and the most famous quotation of the Council."[17] A more complete picture of this incident is this: There was a group of bishops who were vigorously promoting the view that the Pope was above and apart from the Church and that infallibility was his personal attribute. Cardinal Filippo Guidi, a Dominican and a very competent theologian, while speaking on the floor of the council, proposed that the text of the decree should make it clear that, when making infallible decrees, the Pope is not separate from the Church, but speaks in communion with the bishops who are the witnesses of the tradition of their churches. The Pope must speak within the tradition of the Church.

The Pope had personal staff in the council hall who kept him informed of what was happening in the debate. When he learned of Guidi's speech, he was very upset, probably because he thought that Guidi was pushing the idea that the Pope was subordinate to the bishops in the Gallican sense. Thus he ordered Guidi to come to see him at 5 p.m. that very day. When Guidi arrived he saw that the Pope was angry. At the beginning of the conversation, when Guidi mentioned that the Pope must be guided by divine tradition, un-

16. Duffy, *The Tablet*, September 9, 2000.

17. Chadwick, *The Popes and European Revolution*, 210.

der the influence of his anger, the Pope let fly "I am the tradition." Maintaining his calm, Guidi replied that everything he had said was based on St. Thomas and on Bellarmine. With this, the Pope himself calmed down and said, "Certainly, before deciding the Pope must take counsel," and went on to say that he himself had in fact asked the opinion of the bishops prior to the definition of the Immaculate Conception.[18] The unpremeditated outcry of the Pope is not a sign that he was unbalanced so much as that he was living under tremendous pressure. Furthermore, the Pope was reacting to a verbal report of his staff. He had not yet read the actual speech before seeing Guidi.

Another story purporting to show the emotional instability of Pius IX was his alleged violent reaction to a speech given on May 19 by the Melkite Patriarch, Gregory Youssef, urging the Council Fathers to uphold the ancient rights and prerogatives of the Patriarchs of the Eastern Churches. The story is that when he heard of this speech, the Pope sent for Youssef, berated him and even put his foot on Youssef's neck when he bowed before the Pope. However a lengthy and very scholarly article on the Eastern Catholic bishops at Vatican I says this, "We have been unable to find any document to provide historical verification for such treatment by the Pope."[19]In other words, no evidence has ever been found to support this story.

An indication of the basic equilibrium of the Pope is his usual method of arriving at major decisions. The *Syllabus* was under consideration for at least five years. The idea of summoning a council matured over a period of fifteen years. The Pope consulted, prayed, weighed the pros and cons, and took time in reaching major decisions of this kind. All in all, then, there are some well-documented examples which show a man who was mentally and emotionally competent.

---

18. Martina, *Pio IX (1851–1866)*, Vol III, 207.

19. Joseph Hajjar *L'episcopat catholique oriental et le 1er Concile du Vatican* (Revue d'histoire ecclesiastique, 65, 1970) 755 (author's translation). Hajjar was a distinguished scholar, an editor of the journal *Concilium,* and a member of the Belgian Académie Internationale des Sciences Religieuses.

Hasler also impugns the validity of the council on the grounds that the Pope put inordinate pressure on the bishops to endorse his own point of view. It is true that such highly respected historians as Martina and Chadwick do agree that Pius IX did put pressure on the bishops, especially in the last month of the council. For instance, priests and lay people wrote to him complaining about their bishops, who belonged to the council minority and who therefore were opposed to any definition at all, or who at least supported a moderate definition of infallibility. The Pope replied to many of these letters, knowing that at least some of them would become public. In his replies, he congratulated the writers and told them that they were truly loyal to the Holy See and to the faith of the Church. In time, there were so many letters that he could not respond to them all and he gave directions to the Nuncio in Paris that he should reply saying how pleased the Pope was by these letters.[20] He did the same in audiences, praising those with ultramontane convictions and correcting or showing disfavor to those of the minority.[21] Butler reports a letter from the Bishop of Birmingham, William Ullathorne, saying, "The Pope takes every opportunity of impressing his views on the infallibility, both in audiences and in letters that at once get into the papers."[22]

But another way he tried to influence the bishops was his charm, which is described as "extraordinary."[23] He elicited enormous respect, veneration and affection. As a result, the bishops found it very painful to do what they knew would wound him. Butler asks, "What it must have cost men like Rauscher, Haynald, Dupanloup, Melchers, who had enjoyed his affectionate personal friendship, to make their stand against his known wishes, cannot easily be estimated."[24] This personal feeling for Pius IX, together with the reverence of bishops for the office of the Successor of Peter, were certainly factors which

---

20. Butler, *The Vatican Council 1869–1870*, 447.
21. Butler, *The Vatican Council 1869–1870*, 451.
22. Butler, *The Vatican Council 1869–1870*, 446.
23. Butler, *The Vatican Council 1869–1870*, 446.
24. Butler, *The Vatican Council 1869–1870*, 447.

cannot be discounted. But this is not the same as saying that the bishops were not free to vote as they believed.

The fact is that the majority of the bishops wanted the definition. There were nuances in the way they wanted it expressed, ranging from infallibility as a personal prerogative of the Pope to a position that the Pope could only give an infallible decree if it is a statement deriving from divine tradition. Since the majority wanted the definition, they could not be the object of any alleged intimidation on the part of the Pope. But it was not only the majority bishops who wanted the definition. There was widespread popular support for a definition, especially north of the Alps. Schatz says, "This development can only be understood if we remember that ultramontanism responded in large measure to the expectations, desires, and hopes of the Church's 'base', that is, active lay people and particularly the younger clergy. Especially from midcentury onward ultramontanism succeeded in becoming a mass movement."[25] And Alexis de Tocqueville wrote in 1856, "The pope is driven more by the faithful to become absolute ruler of the Church than they are impelled by him to submit to his rule. Rome's attitude is more an effect than a cause."[26]

The question of papal intimidation, then, comes down to whether the minority was truly free to express its views and to vote as it saw fit. Döllinger maintained that the rules of procedure and the action of the presidents made a thorough discussion of the minority's views impossible and that there was not freedom of discussion.[27] Contradicting this, Bishop Ullathorne, a man of independent character, and who, unlike Döllinger, was present in the Council hall, wrote that "Every condition of a full and free debate was satisfied, the question was considered on all its sides both by writing... and by the sifting process of public discussion."[28]

25. Schatz, *Papal Primacy from Its Origins to the Present*, 152.

26. Cited by Schatz, *Papal Primacy from Its Origins to the Present*, 151. Schatz cites this letter of de Tocqueville from Ollivier's work on the Council.

27. Butler, *The Vatican Council 1869–1870*, 459.

28. Butler, *The Vatican Council 1869–1870*, 440.

The American and future cardinal, James Gibbons, the youngest bishop at the council, says that infallibility "was debated with great heat. Never have I heard such plain speaking in my life..."[29]

An indication that the minority was able to vote with freedom is the fact that they made up 20 per-cent of the council membership but gave 40 percent of the speeches on the primacy decree.[30] Another indication of their freedom and that they had an effect on the outcome is that when debate on the primacy decree ended on June 14, there were seventy-two amendments. All but four of these amendments were rejected. Of the four that were accepted, three came from the minority.[31] Bishop David Moriarty of Kerry, a long-time, trusted friend of Newman, wrote to him on October 25, 1870, "I hear some are yet complaining of want of liberty (at the council). This is not fair. The whole conduct of the business was not what some of us had wished; but it was what the immense majority of the Council wished, and the Council cannot complain of its own acts... Even our absence on the last day... was the free act of the Minority..."[32] Butler sums it up this way, "Indeed, if the Vatican Council was not free, it would have to be said that the House of Commons is not free: because freedom of speech is at least as much interfered with by Speaker and members in the latter, as it was by Presidents and Majority bishops in the former."[33] His final judgment is, "When all has been weighed up, the fact stands out that there was no real interference with freedom of speech, or thoroughness of discussion, or independence of voting; and so the ecumenicity of the Vatican Council cannot properly be called in question on the score of defect of liberty."[34]

Then there is the attack on validity because of the claim that since the minority did not take part in the final vote, there was not moral

29. Butler, *The Vatican Council 1869–1870*, 443.

30. Schatz, *Papal Primacy from Its Origins to the Present*, 157.

31. Butler, *The Vatican Council 1869–1870*, 343.

32. Butler, *The Vatican Council 1869–1870*, 444.

33. Butler, *The Vatican Council 1869–1870*, 443.

34. Butler, *The Vatican Council 1869–1870*, 454.

unanimity. This overlooks the fact that in the councils of the first millennium, moral unanimity was regarded as an ideal but not as a strict condition for the validity of a council. "... (A)s a strict condition for the validity of dogmatic conciliar decisions this principle is really quite recent. It was unknown to classical conciliarism and Gallicanism, both of which tended to support the majority principle. Its development begins among the Jansenists of the eighteenth century."[35] The dogmatic decrees were passed by a majority vote which was regarded as sufficient for most of the history of the Church.

But what is to be said of the acceptance of the decrees by the minority?[36] The fact is that within a few months, the greater number of the minority bishops had formally accepted the council. There were some exceptions, such as the Croatian, Strossmayer, who delayed nearly thirteen years before making his formal acceptance, though he had published the decrees in his diocese in 1873. Another member of the minority about whose acceptance there has been some ambiguity is Archbishop Peter Kenrick of St. Louis. However, the fact is that shortly after his return from Rome, in January 1871, he made a public declaration of his acceptance. James Hennessy, who has written in depth about the American bishops at the Council, says of Kenrick, "It may be that Kenrick's thought on the point was confused... but in any event he made it otherwise amply clear that he intended to receive the dogma as it was defined on July 18, and therefore his subjective acceptance of the definition was beyond question."[37] The acceptance by the minority was one of the factors which convinced Newman of the validity of the definition.

Still, Hasler contended that this acceptance by almost all the minority was only pro-forma and not sincere.[38] This is a very grave

---

35. Schatz, *Papal Primacy from Its Origins to the Present*, 157.

36. For an account of the acceptance by the minority bishops see Martina, *Pio IX (1851–1866)*, Vol III, 216–228.

37. James Hennessy, S.J. *The First Council of the Vatican: The American Experience* (New York: Herder and Herder, 1963), 325.

38. Hasler, *How the Pope Became Infallible*, 221–226.

accusation since it means that these bishops violated their own integrity. There is also the question whether Pius IX would have tolerated a merely pro-forma acceptance since what he asked of the bishops was not a statement of acceptance of the decrees, but a profession of faith.

Contrary to Hasler's claim of insincere compliance, the facts show that most of the minority were moved by very good reasons to sincerely accept the decrees of the council. It is true that they voted against the decree on July 11, 1870, but between July 11 and July 18, the date of the solemn final vote, changes and additions were made in the text. They came to see that the additions to the text, such as the quotation from Pope Gregory I and the placing of the doctrine in the context of previous councils, satisfied their concerns that the Pope was not outside the episcopate, that infallibility was not a personal prerogative but a providential care over his solemn, definitive teaching, and that certain conditions were required for infallible decrees. In other words, they came to see that the definition did not teach an open-ended, all-encompassing infallibility which some of the majority had been promoting and so they were able in good conscience to accept it. An example are the French bishops of the minority. "... (T)hose who think that the French minority opposed any concept of infallibility must be corrected."[39] Margaret O'Gara, in her analysis, mentions seven French bishops, including Dupanloup and Darboy of Paris, who held a nuanced doctrine of infallibility even before the council, and she says this "laid the foundation for their subsequent assent to *Pastor aeternus,* when they were able to satisfy themselves that the decree did not fundamentally contradict their earlier understanding of papal infallibility."[40]

Others of the minority were moved by reflecting over time that it was not reasonable to stand against the council when the ma-

39. Margaret O'Gara, *Triumph in Defeat* (Washington, DC: The Catholic University of America Press, 1988), 171

40. O'Gara, *Triumph in Defeat*, 171. See also the review of O'Gara's book by Francis A. Sullivan in *Gregorianum*, Vol 70 (1989) Fasc. 3, 568.

jority of the bishops of the world and large numbers of the faithful accepted the decrees. Quite a number peacefully accepted the decrees by reading Fessler's book, mentioned in Chapter III, and by the strong approbation it received from Pius IX. Some, like the very learned Karl Josef von Hefele, an expert in the history of the councils, explicitly mentioned Fessler's book as one reason which made it possible for him to accept the decrees.[41] This gives some indication that Hasler's claim of insincere acceptance is not well founded.

In the final analysis, just what is the merit of Hasler's position impugning the council? Giacomo Martina is the principal modern biographer of Pius IX, whose work is described by John O'Malley as "a masterly accomplishment, a balanced critical and painstakingly thorough account."[42] Martina evaluates Hasler as having serious defects. "Hasler has the merit of a rich abundance of sources taken from archives all over Europe." But Martina faults Hasler for being selective in his use of sources and of emphasizing negative sources without ever analyzing their accuracy. He passes over the positive testimonies to the Pope and overemphasizes the psychological factors to the detriment of all other factors.[43] He concludes by saying that Hasler is almost uniformly subjective, one-sided and unscientific and that his portrait of Pius IX is more like a caricature.[44] A similar negative appraisal of Hasler was made by the American theologian, John T. Ford, C.S.C., eleven years before Martina's biography of the Pope. He, too, finds that Hasler makes little critical evaluation of his sources and says that "The discrepancies and inconsistencies in Hasler's account strongly suggest that the data has been adroitly arranged

---

41. Hefele had produced a 7-volume history of the councils and had been a professor at Tubingen.

42. John W. O'Malley, *The Beatification of Pope Pius IX* (*America*, August 26–September 2, 2000).

43. Martina, *Pio IX (1851–1866)*, Vol III, 113, n.4.

44. Martina, *Pio IX (1851–1866)*, Vol III, vii.

to fit the thesis."[45] Representative scholars do not find Hasler's attack on the council convincing either. In light of all this, it is reasonable to conclude that there are no solid grounds to call the validity of the council into question.

Another work which treated the freedom of the Council in some depth is *Infallibility on Trial*.[46] The author, Luis Bermejo, after examining a number of approaches to the problem concludes, "In view of all this, does the current position of most Catholic historians and theologians still stand, namely that the freedom of the Council was certainly crippled but sufficient to uphold the validity of the Council's decrees? I think it does."[47]

Notwithstanding his declaration that "This position still holds the field, and at the moment, on the basis of the documentary evidence available so far, there is no cogent reason to abandon it..." Bermejo still maintains that the question of freedom "remains an open question" even though he states that there is no cogent reason to deny freedom.[48] Yves Congar, among the very great scholars of the twentieth century, faults Bermejo on the grounds that he does not distinguish sufficiently between history and historicity and that he does not have an adequate grasp of ecclesiology.[49]

---

45. John T. Ford, C.S.C., *Infallibility: A Review of Recent Studies* (Theological Studies, volume 40, number 2, June 1979), 299. One glaring error of Hasler (106) is that he writes that Giovanni Mastai (Pius IX), on July 4, 1819, received a dispensation to be ordained a priest—the dispensation required because he had had epilepsy. But, in fact, he had been ordained a priest on April 10, 1819.

46. Luis M. Bermejo, S.J., *Infallibility on Trial* (Westminster, MD: Christian Classics, Inc., 1992).

47. Bermejo, S.J., *Infallibility on Trial*, 143.

48. Bermejo S.J., *Infallibility on Trial*, 143. So far as I can determine, Bermejo does not seem to take into account the later work of G. Martina on this point. Bermejo's work was published the same year as Martina's volume on Pius IX, 1867–1878.

49. Yves Congar, *Le Concile Vatican I En Question* (Revue des Sciences Philosophiques et Theologiques, Tome 68, 1984), 450—451.

Chapter VI

NEWMAN AND VATICAN I

It was the *Syllabus of Errors,* promulgated at the end of 1864, which placed the issue of papal infallibility front and center in the public mind, making it a topic of wide interest. This was especially due to its final set of propositions, which were understood to be a condemnation of freedom of religion and the democratic state. A major reason why the prospect of defining papal infallibility was troubling to many was that if papal teaching in the *Syllabus was* to be declared infallible, then in virtue of these final propositions, Catholics could not be loyal citizens of modern democratic states where freedom of religion was a constitutional right. Adding to the growing agitation were William G. Ward, who was vigorously promoting exaggerated ideas of infallibility in the widely read *Dublin Review,* and Archbishop Henry Edward Manning of Westminster, who was promoting a similar point of view. These critiques excited growing concern on the part of the British Government because Ward and Manning were urging, and even campaigning explicitly, that the *Syllabus* should be declared infallible. The government feared uprisings by Catholics because it believed Catholic citizens would be obliged to oppose freedom of religion in England. This fear was not altogether groundless because of the deeper fear that the convergence of sovereign papal primacy, together with infallibility, might embolden the Pope to such acts of authority as those which occurred in centuries past. Lurking in the memory of the government, for example, was the excommunication by Clement VII of Henry VIII and of Queen Elisabeth I by Pius V, both of which were followed by tremendous civil strife and bloodshed.

The prospect that the *Syllabus* might be declared infallible also created serious problems of conscience for devout Catholics who were thoroughly English and devoted to the Crown, and who highly valued religious freedom, as did Catholics in other democratic countries such as the United States of America, where freedom of religion was prized not only for itself but for the positive benefit it was for the life of the Church.

Though exaggerated, ultramontane ideas of papal primacy and infallibility had been circulating during the early part of the century, as we saw in previous chapters. Newman himself did not deal with these issues in any extensive way much before the 1860s. His views about Vatican Council I and infallibility were largely expressed in private letters and in notes he made for his own use. But there were two important exceptions, the *Apologia Pro Vita Sua, which* appeared in 1865, and his *Letter to the Duke of Norfolk*, which appeared in 1875.

But why did this growing agitation affect Newman? The first answer is because Newman had a profound concern for people and was acutely sensitive to what might be injurious or hurtful to them. He had a highly developed pastoral sense. As a Catholic, he wrote about his personal attitude to a forthcoming definition of papal infallibility by stating, "As to myself personally, please God, I do not expect any trial at all." But he went on to speak of ordinary people, "But I cannot help suffering with the various souls which are suffering..."[1] All his life, both as an Anglican and as a Catholic, Newman maintained a strong pastoral involvement with people of all ranks of society. Many of these people came to see him and wrote to him about their problems of conscience. As a result, there is a large body of correspondence in which he discusses papal infallibility and gives advice to a variety of people who were troubled in conscience by the prospect of the conciliar definition.

1. Sheridan Gilley, *Newman and His Age* (London: Darton, Longman and Todd, 1990), 366.

But Newman was not destined to confine his thinking to the private realm for long. Victorian England was a very religious country and there was great public interest in religious questions. In December 1863, a year before the *Syllabus*, something happened which was to lead Newman to a very public expression of his views on the subject of infallibility. It all began with a book review written by Charles Kingsley. Kingsley was an Anglican clergyman, a successful novelist, and a Cambridge professor. He had strong negative feelings against Newman and had been opposed to the Oxford Movement (1833–1845), of which Newman was the leader, particularly through a series of publications called *Tracts for the Times* and through his sermons at the University Church of St. Mary the Virgin in Oxford. The Oxford Movement, in general, was a movement dedicated to the recovery of aspects of the ancient and medieval church, to the defense of church doctrine and to a return to a more sacramental kind of church life. Thus Newman held more frequent services of Holy Communion and heard confessions when asked. The Oxford Movement firmly held that the Church of England was in living continuity with the ancient church of the Fathers, and it held that the Church, as apostolic, had an episcopal form of government, distinguishing the Anglican Church from Protestant Churches which did not have bishops. Another major force giving impetus to the Oxford Movement was Newman's founding of the *Library of the Fathers,* a translation of the works of the Fathers of the Church.[2]

Kingsley's article reviewed a recently published, anti-Catholic work on the history of England by J.A. Froude. In the course of the review, Kingsley mentioned that Newman had little regard for truth, that cunning and deceit were the more important weapons, and that "Truth for its own sake, had never been a virtue with the

2. This return to the sources begun by Newman and a driving force in the Oxford Movement, expanded in the twentieth century and was led by such influential scholars as Jean Danielou, Henri DeLubac, Yves Congar and Lambert Beauduin.

Roman clergy." [3] Clearly he was not an impartial commentator. He was also careless. "Some of Kingsley's charges were based on slipshod paraphrases of Newman's words."[4]

Newman took Kingsley's review to mean that a Catholic professed doctrines which he could not possibly believe in his heart, "that I also believe in the existence of a power on earth, which of its own will imposes on men any new set of credenda when it pleases by a claim of infallibility; in consequence, that my own thoughts are not my own property..."[5] Newman thus understands Kingsley to be saying that the Catholic is essentially a mental slave, that the infallible authority of the Church touches all subjects, in that it is universal, absolute and unconditional, arbitrary and capricious.

In fact, Newman had never said what Kingsley imputed to him and both he and Richard Holt Hutton, Anglican editor of *The Spectator,* assailed Kingsley vigorously. They both emphasized the fact that the Newman sermon, which Kingsley used to attack his Catholic views, was preached when he was an Anglican and thus could not honorably be used to impugn Newman's thought as a Catholic. There followed several exchanges between Newman and Kingsley, but Kingsley remained intransigent. As a result, Newman felt he had no choice but to publish his correspondence with Kingsley. This in turn led Kingsley to publish a pamphlet, *What, then, does Dr. Newman mean?* This pamphlet, and the fact that Kingsley never rose above half-truths and falsehood in his attacks, finally led Newman to the firm decision to write publicly to defend his own integrity. What particularly stung him was Kingsley's claim that Newman was not a sincere Anglican before his conversion, and that he was a "papist" for years prior to being received into communion with the Holy See. "The whole strength of what he says... lies in the antecedent prejudice that I was a Papist while

---

3. Ker, *John Henry Newman*, 533.

4. Gilley, *Newman and His Age*, 324–325.

5. John Page, *What Will Dr. Newman Do?* (Collegeville, MN: Liturgical Press, 1994), 20.

I was an Anglican."[6] And in the preface to the second edition of the *Apologia*, he writes, "There has been a general feeling that I was for years . . . a 'Romanist' in Protestant livery and service; that I was doing the work of a hostile Church in the bosom of the English Establishment, and knew it, or ought to have known it."[7] The rumors kept growing, culminating in the claim that "I had actually been received into that religion (the Catholic Church), and . . . had leave given me to profess myself a Protestant still. Others went even further, and gave it out to the world, as a matter of fact . . . that I was actually a Jesuit."[8] It was these intolerable accusations of duplicity, more than the need to defend the doctrine of infallibility, which led to the writing of the Apologia *Pro Vita Sua*, with its subtitle *Being a History of His Religious Opinions*. In other words, he did not envision the *Apologia* so much as a defense of doctrine as a forthright and accurate history of the development of his own personal religious convictions.

But there was another set of troubling accusations coming not from Anglicans but from ultramontane Catholics. They accused him of being weak in Catholic faith because he did not support their exaggerated ideas of an all-encompassing and personal infallibility of the Pope. "If his treatment by Protestants was painful however, that which Newman received for a time from Catholics, including some of his fellow converts was even more so, until it culminated in his almost morbid streak of depression in the early 1860s."[9] The sadness and depression were due to the shabby treatment he had received during these years, combined with mounting rumors that he was having increasing doubts about his conversion.

6. Ker, *John Henry Newman*, 542.

7. John Henry Newman, *Apologia Pro Vita Sua* (ed. Martin J. Svaglic, Oxford at the Clarendon Press 1967), 9. All citations of the *Apologia* will be made from the Svaglic edition.

8. *Apologia*, 9. For more on this see Peter L'Estrange *Newman's Relations with the Jesuits* (Heythrop Journal XXIX 1988), 58.

9. *Apologia*, Editor's Introduction xii.

The fact is that there was a cumulus of regrettable experiences which contributed to his gloomy frame of mind. He had been asked to set up a Catholic University in Ireland and threw himself and his own financial resources into the project, but was thwarted by some Irish bishops who wanted the university to be a sort of lay seminary, rather than a university in the true sense, and so he had to abandon the project. Then, in 1853, there were unbearable strains between the Oratory in Birmingham and the London Oratory, as a result of which Newman felt that the London Oratory had damaged his reputation in Rome and among English Catholics.[10]

Then, in 1857, the English Bishops under the leadership of Cardinal Wiseman asked Newman to make a new translation of the Bible. But after Newman had spent money and time getting the project started, Wiseman abandoned it, which, not surprisingly, led Newman to think that Wiseman no longer trusted him. In 1859, at the request of his own bishop, Ullathorne, and of Cardinal Wiseman, Newman accepted editorship of the *Rambler.*[11] Not long after assuming this responsibility, he published an article entitled *On Consulting the Faithful in Matters of Doctrine.* In the course of the article, he made reference to the part the laity played in the Arian controversy of the fourth century. Large numbers of the laity held firm to the true doctrine of the divinity of Christ, but many bishops wavered or embraced Arianism. Newman held that it was the laity who saved the Church at a moment when the functions of the bishops were temporarily suspended. He was quickly denounced to Rome for heresy.

Another factor which caused him concern was the interpretation being given to his suspected opposition to the temporal power of

10. *Apologia*, Editor's Introduction, xiv.

11. *The Rambler* was a magazine published over some twenty years by Catholic laymen and dealing with Catholic topics including doctrinal issues. Newman assumed editorship for a short time. The magazine ceased publication in 1868, mostly due to opposition from the British bishops.

the Pope as ruler of the Papal States. Monsignor Talbot, [12]English convert and trusted member of the Papal household in Rome, was author of a rumor that Newman had actually contributed money to Garibaldi's campaign to seize Rome and unify Italy[13] and had declared that "Newman is the most dangerous man in England."[14] At this time, there was a groundswell of vigorous support for a beleaguered Pope who had long been under attack for his doctrinal teachings, particularly in the *Syllabus*, and who was now threatened with losing the last vestiges of his political independence thanks to the movement to unify Italy, which was allied with a strong anticlerical element. Anyone who was not enthusiastic in support of retaining the Papal States was thought weak in faith. A redoubtable factor reinforcing this attitude, the *Syllabus* condemned the idea that the suppression of the civil power of the Pope would be a great blessing and bring great benefit to the Church.[15] Newman also feared that Ward, Manning and others were vigorously working to "bring in a new theory of Papal Infallibility, which would make it a mortal sin, to be visited by damnation, not to hold the Temporal Power necessary to the Papacy."[16] Newman was convinced that Manning, Ward and Monsignor Talbot really considered themselves to be the Church.[17] In very sharp language, Newman rejected the tendency to turn everything into a dogma of the faith: "... I would observe that, while I acknowledge one Pope '*iure divino*,' I acknowledge no other,

12. George Talbot, a convert to the Catholic Church in 1843, who lived in Rome, was made a Papal Chamberlain and was greatly trusted by Pius IX. He was an extreme Ultramontane and hostile to Newman. Edward Short describes Talbot as "An ecclesiastical troublemaker par *excellence*" and mentions that in 1868, Talbot was sent to an asylum in France where he died. See Edward Short, *Newman and His Contemporaries* (New York: T&T Clark International, 2011), 424.
13. Ker, *John Henry Newman*, 560.
14. Gilley, *Newman and His* Age, 348.
15. *Syllabus*, 76, Denziger 2976.
16. Gilley, *Newman and His* Age, 349.
17. Gilley, *Newman and His* Age, 349.

and that I think it a usurpation, too wicked to be comfortably dwelt upon, when individuals use their own private judgment, in the discussion of religious questions, not simply *'abundare in suo sensu'* but for the purpose of anathematizing the private judgement of others."[18]

So, all in all, he felt increasingly afflicted, isolated and rejected, "fading out from the world and having nothing to do with its interests or affairs."[19] And he wrote, "...I am noticing all this opposition and distrust...because they have...succeeded in destroying my influence and my usefulness. Persons who would naturally look towards me, converts who would naturally come to me, inquirers who would naturally consult me, are stopped by some light or unkind word said against me. I am passé, in decay; I am untrustworthy..."[20] Reports of Newman's despondency were circulating, and, in July 1862, they reached a climax when it was openly reported in two newspapers that he had left the Oratory and was actually in the process of returning to the Church of England.[21] "Reports gradually magnified in the telling, and in July 1862 it was openly stated in the *Stamford Morning Advertiser* – the paragraph being also reproduced in the *Globe* newspaper – that he had left the 'Brompton Oratory' and was going to return to the Church of England."[22]

If the accusations of Kingsley led to the writing of the *Apologia,* it was the charge that he was wavering and disillusioned with the Catholic Church, which was a significant influence on the tone and content of its final chapter. This background explains why

18. Gilley, *Newman and His* Age, 170. The violent and unfounded attacks on Newman's orthodoxy bring to mind the same kind of attacks visited with such fervor on the truly premiere Catholic scholar and exemplary priest, Raymond Brown.

19. *Apologi,* Editor's Introduction xvi.

20. *Apologia*, Editor's Introduction xvii.

21. Wilfrid Ward, *The Life Of John Henry Cardinal Newman,* Vol. I (London: Longmans, Green, And Co., 1913), 579.

22. Ward, *The Life Of John Henry Cardinal Newman,* 579.

he begins the final chapter with this declaration: "From the time that I became a Catholic... I have had no variations to record, and have had no anxiety of heart whatever. I have been in perfect peace and contentment; I have never had one doubt... it was like coming into port after a rough sea; and my happiness on that score remains to this day without interruption."[23] These words are a firm denial of any wavering on his part about his conversion, a rejection of the rumors which had been circulating, and a repudiation of the published reports of his return to the Church of England.

When he comes to the subject of infallibility in the *Apologia,* it is not a comment on the dogmatic decree of the Council, which was still five years away. Rather he treats infallibility with a view to explaining how the Church's claim to teach infallibly does not make him a mental slave or mean that he publicly subscribes to teachings which he does not sincerely believe in his heart. Of note, too, is that he does not focus on the infallibility of the Pope in the *Apologia* but rather the infallibility of the Church. "... I am here not determining any thing about the essential seat of that power (infallibility) because that is a question doctrinal, not historical and practical."[24] In chapter 5, then, he explains that he can be sincere in accepting the infallible teaching of the Church because, for one thing, it is confined to the religious realm, limited and not all encompassing. It does not extend "beyond religious opinion."

He lays the foundation for his treatment of infallibility by stating the basic principle that despite its tremendous gifts and poten-

---

23. *Apologia*, 214.

24. *Apologia*, 223. One reason why he did not bring up papal infallibility here was that he, and many theologians at that time, regarded it as a theological opinion and not a matter of what he calls "Catholic doctrine." Inasmuch as he is here defending "Catholic doctrine," he did not think it appropriate to introduce theological opinions. See C.S. Dessain, *An Unpublished Paper by Cardinal Newman on the Development of Doctrine* in *The Journal of Theological Studies* (October 1958) n.s. ix, pt. 2, 329–330.

tial, human nature is in some way wounded as the condition of the world shows. Neither humanity nor the world is now in that state of perfection which it enjoyed at the time of the original creation described in the Book of Genesis. "The human race is implicated in some terrible aboriginal calamity."[25] And he adds, "...And thus the doctrine of what is theologically called original sin becomes to me almost as certain as that the world exists, and as the existence of God."[26] The ability of the human mind to discover religious truth, though not extinguished, is definitely impaired. As a result, the human mind naturally tends to disbelieve and, often, to distort what religious truth it can discover. Because of this "terrible aboriginal calamity," there is a certain imbalance, even a kind of darkness, which the human mind experiences. And so there is a need for an infallible authority to challenge the wild excesses of the human mind.[27] Although the human intellect of its nature can arrive at religious truth, in the present state of things there is the tendency of the intellect to simple unbelief and he speaks of "the all-corroding, all-dissolving skepticism of the intellect."[28] He has in mind not simply the individual human person who is seeking religious truth, but humanity as such. He then remarks that the remedies alleged to counter this destructive force of human reason left to itself, the State church and the Bible, cannot of themselves accomplish the task of preserving religious truth. Newman had witnessed that the State Church in England had been unable to withstand the influences of skepticism and of political expediency, as in the case of the

---

25. It is interesting that this truth was touched on by the columnist, David Brooks, in the *New York Times*, April 17, 2015, "What's lost is the more balanced view, that we are splendidly endowed but also broken...The romantic culture of self-glorification has to be balanced with an older philosophic tradition, based on the realistic acknowledgement that we are all made of crooked timber..."

26. *Apologia*, 218, 4.

27. He is postulating an infallible authority in connection with religious truth, not in connection with any other areas of truth.

28. *Apologia*, 218, 19.

Jerusalem bishopric,[29] which caused him such anguish. The state Church is, as its name conveys, under the authority of the state, the monarch or parliament. As for the Bible, no book is self-interpreting. And so Newman writes, "Experience proves surely that the Bible does not answer a purpose for which it was never intended. It may be accidentally the means of the conversion of individuals; but a book, after all, cannot make a stand against the wild living intellect of man..."[30] Newman therefore concludes that the conflict between the claims of reason and religion is resolved through "the Church's infallibility, as a provision, adapted by the mercy of the Creator, to preserve religion in the world, and to restrain that freedom of thought, which of course in itself is one of the greatest of our natural gifts, and to rescue it from its own suicidal excesses."[31] So he postulates infallibility for the Church because fallen human nature, despite its gifts, cannot in its existing state preserve or attain these religious truths and needs a force to challenge it and direct it into the correct path. All this argument is based on the assumption that if God gave a revelation, he would make provision for its preservation. The human mind, of itself, in fact, does not preserve divine truth, the state church does not preserve it, and the Bible by itself is not a remedy for the deficiencies of the human intellect. And so the need for a divinely given living power to challenge the human intellect, to call it to account, and to preserve the divinely given revelation. This is the thesis.

He goes on to point out that such infallible authority is not omnicompetent. It has for its object only religious truths or those having a necessary connection to it and does not extend to political or

---

29. The British Government had made an arrangement whereby the Anglican Bishop in Jerusalem would also have pastoral care for Protestants there. This was a severe problem for Newman because the German Protestants did not have an Episcopal Church structure. See *The Oxford Dictionary of the Christian Church, Third Edition*, ed. F.L. Cross, E.A. Livingstone (New York: Oxford University Press, 1997), Jerusalem Anglican Bishopric, 869-870.

30. *Apologia*, 219, 31–35.

31. *Apologia*, 220, 12–17.

scientific issues as such. He affirms that infallible teaching regarding religious truths is not a major difficulty for believers because when the Church infallibly teaches these things, "...it is but expressing what any good Catholic, of fair ability though unlearned, would say himself, from common and sound sense if the matter could be put before him."[32] Newman thus affirms that most Catholics do not find it difficult to accept infallible teaching because it must always be a teaching which is contained in the deposit of faith and most often is something that has for a long time been generally held. He uses the examples of the Immaculate Conception and of how Pius IX spent some years working through a commission to study the long history of the Church and teaching of the Fathers, as well as the practice and belief of ordinary Catholics. When the dogmatic definition was made in 1854, the whole Church accepted it peacefully. And so he concludes that far from making the Catholic a mental slave, "Infallibility cannot act outside a definite circle of thought...The great truths of the moral law, of natural religion, and of Apostolical faith, are both its boundary and its foundation. It must not go beyond them, and it must ever appeal to them...And it must ever profess to be guided by Scripture and by tradition. Nothing can be imposed on me different in kind from what I hold already, much less contrary to it."[33]

In speaking of infallibility in the *Apologia*, Newman, as mentioned, had explicitly said that he was not attending to the "essential seat of that power." That is, he is speaking of the infallibility of the Church as such and not touching on who, in the Church, has that prerogative. In fact, he asserts that a basic reason why objectors attack the infallibility of the Pope is that they cannot admit that the Church can teach with true and binding authority. Speaking of Gladstone's attack, he says, "It is not the existence of a Pope, but of a Church, which is his aversion."[34] The *Apologia*

32. *Apologia*, 230, 12–15.

33. *Apologia* 227, 3–16.

34. Ker, *John Henry Newman*, 687, footnote 160.

therefore does not treat the subject of papal infallibility as such. Newman states that he, personally, is not troubled by the idea of an infallible church, which is necessary for the preservation of revealed truth.

His most extensive treatment of Vatican I is found in a lengthy work called *A Letter Addressed to His Grace the Duke of Norfolk.*[35] The *Letter*, published five years after the Council, in 1875, was occasioned by a fiery pamphlet, authored by William Gladstone, until recently Prime Minister of England. Gladstone denounced Rome for substituting "for the proud boast of *semper eadem*[36] a policy of violence and change in faith... when no one can become her convert, without renouncing his moral and mental freedom, and placing his civil loyalty and duty at the mercy of another; when she has equally repudiated modern thought and ancient history."[37] A basic idea running through much of what Gladstone wrote was that the Council had made Catholics the political slaves of the Pope and, in secular matters, they owed obedience to the Pope and not to the Queen.[38] Much of this shows how deeply Gladstone's hostile attitude was influenced by the *Syllabus*.

Two people in particular influenced Gladstone's negative thinking. One was his friend Döllinger, who, in the very words used by Gladstone, had said that Vatican I meant "a policy of change in faith,"[39] implying that by the decrees on primacy and infallibility, the constitution of the Church was being changed so that the Pope absorbed all the powers of the bishops and that bishops were only legates of the Pope.

---

35. Newman, *Duke of Norfolk*, 175.

36. This expression means always the same, unchangeable. It was used by Gregory XVI, (see c.1, p.8 above) earlier in the century and was especially dear to the Ultramontanes.

37. Gilley, *Newman and His* Age, 372–373. Gilley adds the comment that theological pursuits were the main interest of Gladstone's life.

38. Gilley, *Newman and His* Age, 373.

39. Gilley, *Newman and His* Age, 373.

The second person contributing to Gladstone's hostility was his friend of Oxford days, Archbishop Henry Edward Manning. In October 1870, three months after the definition, Manning published a pastoral letter in which he ascribed to the Council exaggerated interpretations of infallibility.[40] "Typically, Manning's pastoral letter in October gave the exaggerated impression that the Pope's infallibility was unlimited."[41] Manning also, as previously mentioned, actively promoted the idea that the *Syllabus* should be defined at the Council. Gladstone thus cannot be entirely faulted for his belief that the Council, by its teaching on infallibility and primacy, was endorsing the doctrine of the *Syllabus* and that Catholics would be obliged to oppose freedom of religion and to reject the modern democratic state.

Gladstone had served sixty years in the House of Commons and led four Governments as Prime Minister.[42] Given his prestige and the virulence of his language, there was an overwhelming sentiment among British Catholics for the need of a public response, and the choice for that response was Newman, who was universally believed to be the most distinguished Catholic capable of succeeding at the task. This was also a turning point for Newman personally, since this request, having to do with a matter of such public and critical importance, showed that there was a positive opinion of him as one of the few who could make a truly pivotal contribution.

The response took the literary form of a letter addressed to the Duke of Norfolk. Several interesting things lay behind the choice of the Duke as the addressee of this Letter. For one thing, he had been a pupil at the Oratory school and thus was well known to Newman. But the choice of the Duke of Norfolk, member of a pre-Reformation Catholic family, was in its way a subtle declara-

---

40. Henry Edward Manning *The Vatican Council and its Definitions: A Pastoral Letter to the Clergy* (London, 1870).

41. Ker, *John Henry Newman*, 658–659.

42. Short, *Newman and His Contemporaries*, 218.

tion of how absurd Gladstone's attack on Catholics was, because in effect he was saying that the premiere Duke and Earl Marshal of England could not be a loyal citizen.[43]

In the *Letter*, then, contradicting the broad claims of Gladstone, Newman established the fundamental truth that the infallibility of the Church and of the Pope is limited in its object and constrained by its circumstance. Only that definition is infallible which is directed to the universal church and concerns a divinely revealed truth contained in the revelation given to the Church. In some detail and with convincing power, Newman eliminated Gladstone's objection to the Vatican Council decrees by explaining their moderate and limited scope. He insisted that infallibility was not a personal, arbitrary quality of the Pope. In a note, he quoted Fessler's book, so enthusiastically praised by Pius IX, "The Pope is not infallible as a man, or a theologian, or a priest, or a bishop, or a temporal prince, or a judge or a legislator, or in his political views, or even in his government of the Church."[44] He echoes this same moderation in a private letter dated seven days after the promulgation of the decrees: "I saw the new definition yesterday, and am pleased by its moderation—that is if the doctrine in question is to be defined at all. The terms are vague and comprehensive; and, personally, I have no difficulty in admitting it."[45] Thus it is not surprising that Newman would understand the papal prerogative of infallible teaching not "to be of every-day use, but...as a protection or remedy in great emergencies or on supreme occasions, when nothing else will serve, as extraordinary and solemn acts of her (the Church's) religious sovereignty."[46] Newman asserted the principle of authority

---

43. Gilley, *Newman and His* Age, 374.

44. Newman, *Duke of Norfolk,* 325 n. 3. Newman used two versions of Fessler's book. One was an English translation made by Ambrose St. John, one of Newman's close friends and a member of the Birmingham Oratory. The other was a French translation published in 1873.

45. *Duke of Norfolk,* 301.1.

46. *Duke of Norfolk,* 209.1.

while, at the same time, asserting its limited scope. Infallibility was understood by Newman as an emergency power.

Then Newman went on to take up the problem of authority and conscience. Gladstone seemed to imply that an infallible authority extinguished conscience. The Catholic, subject to papal infallible authority, would have to deny his conscience, which might dictate otherwise. The treatment of conscience in the *Letter* is among the great Catholic treatises on the subject. Newman distinguishes between papal authority, which articulates general religious truths, and conscience, which makes the judgment that this single individual act should or should not be done. Thus, the infallible teaching office would be concerned with broad truths such as these: Jesus Christ was crucified and died for the redemption of the whole world, and that the crucified and risen Lord is truly, and not merely symbolically, present in the Sacrament of the Eucharist. On the other hand, conscience is not concerned with general religious truth and is not a teacher of truth. Conscience is concerned with individual acts. Newman made an additional distinction between the Pope defining revealed truth infallibly and the Pope giving various kinds of disciplinary directives to be observed in the Church.

Gladstone was not focused on the problem of dogma but rather was ascribing infallibility to papal orders or directives. He erroneously believed that Vatican I had taught that the Pope is infallible in all his acts and directives,[47] and that in view of this, a Catholic would be obliged to obey a directive from the Pope, such as an order to kidnap Queen Victoria or a papal command to throw a bomb into the Houses of Parliament. Newman strongly rejected this view of papal authority. And in this connection he says, "I am far from saying that Popes are never in the wrong... I am not bound to defend the policy or acts of particular Popes..."[48] In a note, he supported this distinction by making reference to the criticism which Pope Urban VIII brought against Clement VII and

47. Gilley, *Newman and His* Age, 375.

48. *Duke of Norfolk*, 217.5.

Pius V for the excommunications of Henry VIII and Elisabeth I. Of these acts, Pope Urban says, "We bewail it with tears of blood."[49] Even Popes criticized other Popes.

Another distinguished theologian, Joseph Ratzinger, says this, "...(F)or Newman, conscience represents the inner complement and limit of the Church principle. Over the pope as the expression of the binding claim of ecclesiastical authority there still stands one's own conscience, which must be obeyed before all else, if necessary even against the requirement of ecclesiastical authority."[50] Several things must be said here. First, conscience, according to both Newman and Ratzinger, is not a teacher of objective truth but a subjective, personal judgment about what one must do here and now. Hence to assert the primacy of conscience does not mean that one's personal judgment of conscience is correct or true. Conscience is not the teacher of objective truth. In addition, this teaching on conscience does not mean to exalt a subjective approach to truth or morality. But it does envision and presume that the individual makes a genuine, and even laborious, effort to embrace the teaching of church authority. For Newman, then, the Catholic is not a mental slave before the power of an infallible church because, for one thing, infallibility is a prerogative limited to revealed truth. Secondly, neither the Pope nor the Church is infallible in policy or disciplinary decrees.

Though he publicly rejected the objections of Kingsley and Gladstone, nevertheless for reasons different from theirs, prior to the actual Council, Newman did have his own reservations about what it was rumored to be considering. To understand his point of view, we must recall that before the dogmatic definitions of the Council, it was not clear what the Council would actually teach. And given the secrecy which covered the Council's deliberations, there was really no accurate knowledge of what was taking place. Ward was

49. Letter 217, note 2.

50. Joseph Ratzinger, *The Dignity of the Human Person* (New York: Herder & Herder, *Commentary on the Documents of Vatican II*, 1969), 134.

writing his articles, Manning was pushing for a definition of the *Syllabus,* Acton was writing his reports based on personal contacts in Rome, Döllinger in Germany was publishing his own negative articles against the Council based on reports he had from Acton in Rome. So it is understandable that in this climate, Newman would have reasons for grave fears about what might emerge from the Council. These reasons he did not express in public but in private letters. So in the first place, in the absence of accurate information, Newman's reservations about the Council were understandable.

But Newman had other reasons for opposing the definition of papal infallibility by Vatican Council I. He held that in the history of the Church, doctrines had not been defined unless they had been attacked. He did not think that there was any widespread controversy over the papal authority to make decisions about the doctrine of infallibility. He believed with other theologians that the Pope had in fact taught infallibly in the case of the condemnation of Jansenism by Pius VI in 1794. Even so, Newman was in the mainstream of theological thinking at the time in believing that papal infallibility was an open question. He says "It is hardly mentioned till the time of the Jansenist controversy"[51] and adds "Common sense tells us that what was an open question 30 years ago is an open question now."[52] When he says that "it was an open question 30 years ago," he is alluding to discussions between leading Irish bishops and the British government regarding Catholic Emancipation, which was to be enacted in 1829.[53] One

51. J. Derek Holmes, ed., *The Theological Papers of John Henry Newman on Biblical Inspiration and Infallibility* (Oxford: Clarendon Press, 1979), 150.

52. *Holmes, ed., The Theological Papers of John Henry Newman,* 103.

53. Cardinal Consalvi, Secretary of State to Pius VII, went to England in July 1814 before the Congress of Vienna where he discussed Catholic emancipation in some depth with the Foreign Minister, Lord Castlereagh. One sticking point was the oath of loyalty to the Crown, which Catholics would have to take. Consalvi thought that the issue of the oath could be satisfactorily resolved. See John Martin Robinson, *Cardinal Consalvi* (London: Bodley Head, 1987), 104–105.

issue in these discussions was papal infallibility and how that could affect the loyalty of Irish citizens. "The Irish bishops were able to give assurances, presumably with the approbation of Rome, that Catholics were not obliged to hold the infallibility of the Pope."[54] The Irish bishops published a lengthy statement dated January 25, 1826, in which they emphatically deny any power to the Pope over the civil and political affairs of the British Isles and they declared "true allegiance to our most gracious sovereign lord King George the Fourth." They forthrightly state "that it is not an article of the Catholic faith, neither are they (the Catholics of Ireland) required to believe, that the pope is infallible..."[55] There are archival indications that Rome was following the Irish Bishops' work on their statement.[56] As a matter of fact, the Sacred Penitentiary in 1820, and again in 1831, "had declared that the Gallican doctrine, though reprobated by the Holy See, had never incurred any theological censure, and therefore could be held as a free opinion..."[57] Yet Newman himself said repeatedly, "I have never been against the

54. J. Page, "What Will Newman Do," 29.

55. *Declaration of the Archbishops and Bishops of the Roman Catholic Church in Ireland.* The text of the *Declaration* is found in James Doyle, *An Essay on the Catholic Claims* (London: J. Booker, 1826), 300–301. This *Declaration* was unanimous and signed by all the bishops of Ireland. Forty-four years later, at the Council itself, Bishop John MacEvilly of Galway referred to this 1826 declaration of the Irish bishops and declared forthrightly, "I also...make the same declaration..." See Butler, *The Vatican Council 1869–1870*, 310.

56. On December 18, 2015, I received (Prot. N. 4160/15) correspondence from the Congregation for the Evangelization of Peoples, which contains the English version of the Irish Bishops' statement of January 1826. But it also contains an Italian translation of the Statement, which indicates that it was under study in the Congregation. I would conclude from this that the Congregation was clearly aware of what the Irish Bishops were saying and did not prevent them from publishing it. This means that on the issue of the infallibility of the Pope, Newman's judgment that it was still an open question in 1826 is well founded.

57. Butler, *The Vatican Council 1869–1870*, 310–311. Butler does not give the source for this information.

Pope's infallibility."[58] It was not the infallibility he opposed but the *definition* of infallibility. He was opposed to the definition on the grounds that it was moving too fast, "He continued to be shocked by what he considered the haste of the proceedings at Rome..."[59] He contended that there should be more time for theologians to debate the issue.

In September 1869, a few months before the opening of the Council, he added in his personal notes some other reasons, among them that a definition would only lead to new controversies and contentions. He believed that the resulting controversies would last long into the future.[60]

Still another reason for his opposition tothe definition was the likelihood that papal primacy would be defined in terms of sovereignty. If the Pope is an absolute sovereign, above and outside the rest of the Church, and he also has an infallible teaching power, Newman feared that this concentration of power would give rise to arbitrary and ill-advised acts of authority that would make the Pope less willing to listen to the Church. Ian Ker, author of a magisterial biography of Newman, writes, "Towards the end of November (1869) he put down on paper his considered objections to the threatened definition...A definition would lead not only to enormous controversy, but also 'to an alteration of the *elementary constitution* of the Church', because it would encourage the Pope to act alone without the bishops. Finally, because any definition would be a 'retrospective doctrine', it would bring up a host of difficult questions about past papal teachings. 'If any thing', he concluded bitterly, 'could throw religion into confusion, make skeptics, encourage scoffers, and throw back inquirers, it will be the defini-

58. Holmes, ed., *The Theological Papers of John Henry Newman*, 103.

59. J. Page, "What Will Newman Do," 402.

60. J. Page, "What Will Newman Do," 401. A recent article touches on this point of controversy. See Mark E. Powell, *The "Patient and Fraternal Dialog" on Papal Infallibility: Contributions of a Free-Church Theologian* in *Theological Studies*, March 2013, Vol 74, n. 1, 112–113.

tion of this doctrine.' Any definition would be 'most unseasonable and unwise'.[61]

After the Council, Newman's great testimonial and witness to his own faith and acceptance of the Council was his *Letter to the Duke of Norfolk*. The *Letter* was a statement as well of the authentic meaning of the decrees and a repudiation of the extreme interpretations given before and after the Council by Manning and Ward. Consonant with the Council decrees, Newman did not understand papal infallibility as a wide-ranging prerogative. He did not understand it as a power frequently used by the Pope, but as an emergency power to be reserved for critical situations. He explicitly states this in the *Letter* as mentioned on page xxx of this chapter, where he says that the infallible teaching function is "not to be of every-day use" but "in great emergencies." A distinguished modern theologian and official of the Roman Curia, Cardinal Walter Kasper, has expressed the same position. He says that the decrees of the bishops at Vatican I "were especially conceived for extreme and exceptional situations."[62] Some of Newman's fears about what might happen were never realized and we saw that after he had read the text of the actual definition, he was reassured.

61. Ker, *John Henry Newman*, 635.

62. Kasper, *The Petrine Ministry*, 19.

Chapter VII

CONCLUDING REFLECTIONS ON THE COUNCIL

The outbreak of the Franco-Prussian War on July 19, 1870, led to the adjournment of Vatican Council I, which in fact was never resumed. However, in its fourth and final session, on July 18, it defined the dogmas of the primacy of jurisdiction and infallible magisterium of the Pope. There were grave fears about the negative effect of a definition of infallibility—that it would lead to apostasies, that the prestige and influence of the Pope would be diminished, and that the Pope would be ridiculed. Döllinger, for instance, had predicted that a question would be submitted to Rome by telegram and in a matter of hours the answer in the form of a dogmatic definition would be telegraphed to the inquirer.[1] Yet those fears and ominous expectations have not been realized. While infallibility was and even continues to be a great preoccupation, this is largely due to an exaggerated, fundamentalist understanding of infallibility. When infallibility is divorced from its doctrinal and theological foundations, its scope and location within the infallibility of the Church, and as a function of primacy, a caricature of infallibility is created that is in conflict with what Vatican I taught.

In fact, since Vatican I, papal primacy has in many ways played a stronger role in the life of the Church than has papal

1. Schatz, *Papal Primacy From Its Origins to the Present,* 167 (he cites Janus *Der Papst und das Concil von Janus* Leipzig, 1869 – 51–52) English: The Pope and the Council by Janus (Boston: Roberts, 1870).

infallibility.[2] For instance, since 1870, infallibility has been invoked only once, in 1950, when Pope Pius XII defined the bodily assumption of the Blessed Virgin Mary. But if infallible definitions are manifestly rare, the ordinary or non-infallible teaching of the Pope has greatly increased since 1870. This is seen in the multiple use of the encyclical as an instrument of teaching, beginning with Pope Leo XIII, who was elected in 1878. Most of the encyclicals before Leo were condemnatory or limiting in nature, such as *Quanta cura* of Pius IX. But since Leo XIII, encyclicals usually have been more positive in character, giving positive directions or calling to new frontiers of action. Examples of such encyclicals are *Rerum novarum* of Leo XIII on the rights of labor, *Mediator Dei* of Pius XII on the Liturgy, and *Pacem in terris* of Pope John XXIII on peace and justice in a world moving toward globalization. These encyclicals had powerful and wide-spread effects everywhere in the world but they were neither intended nor understood as dogmatic or infallible declarations. Since 1870 the popes have dealt with the real questions of dogma, morals, and social teaching not by infallible dogmatic definitions but by the ordinary papal magisterium.[3] Vatican I did not treat the ordinary magisterium of the Pope,[4] and so that topic does not come within the framework of this book. I mention it as an illustration of how the general preoccupation and fascination with infallibility has tended to diminish focus on papal primacy, which in many ways has had a more powerful effect than the exercise of the infallible

2. Schatz, *Papal Primacy From Its Origins to the Present,* 166.

3. Schatz, *Papal Primacy From Its Origins to the Present,* 167.

4. It is not true to say that unless a teaching is defined, it is not binding. This, for one thing, would mean that most of the teaching of the Church is not binding since relatively little has been defined. It is important to note that even within this vast area of non-defined Church teaching, there are levels of teaching which must be taken into consideration. For more on this topic, see Francis A.Sullivan, S.J., *Creative Fidelity* (Mahwah, NJ: Paulist Press, 1996), 23–24. See also Karl Rahner, *Magisterium,*Sacramentum Mundi, Vol III, (New York: Herder, 1969), 351–358.

magisterium.[5] Even so, the infallibility decree of Vatican I, correctly understood, limited in its object and surrounded by conditions, provides a necessary and important anchor, particularly in confused and troubled moments. It is one of the gifts of Vatican I to the Church that doctrinal turmoil and confusion do not have to go on without end. In the roiling tempest of a Church in distress, the Risen One is present in His Church to assist his Vicar to speak the word of calm and guide the company of believers to the shore in a crisis. Infallibility, then, is a function of the ministry of unity and falls within the horizon of primacy as one of the means of preserving the Church in unity of faith and communion when circumstances warrant it.

I have cited Newman in these pages because he is such an unimpeachable scholar and a powerful exemplar of one of the preeminent qualities of the Catholic theologian, faith seeking understanding. Newman was also unwavering in asserting the indispensability of history for a correct understanding of doctrine. Equally strong was his conviction about the development of doctrine. He clearly understood that revealed truth is an inexhaustible treasure whose depths remain ever to be discovered anew and, consequently, he saw that if fundamental revealed truths such as the Trinity and the Incarnation underwent development, then the primacy and its attributes have undergone development and can be known more deeply, and can be expressed and understood in new and broadened perspectives. In fact, so important was his conviction about development that Newman would write, "I never should have been a Catholic had I not received the doctrine of the development of dogmas."[6]

---

5. A thorough treatment of the ordinary papal magisterium can be found in Francis A. Sullivan, S.J., *Magisterium* (Dublin: Gill and Macmillan, 1983), 119–152.

6. Charles Dessain, Ed., *The Letters and Diaries of John Henry Newman*, Vol 23–31, 1973–1977 (Oxford: Clarendon Press), *Letter to Alfred Plummer, 3 April 1871. 25: 308–310.*

The knowledge of history and the consciousness of doctrinal development are incompatible with doctrinal fundamentalism. The Pontifical Biblical Commission called fundamentalism a form of intellectual suicide: "... (F)undamentalism actually invites people to a kind of intellectual suicide. It injects into life a false certitude, for it unwittingly confuses the divine substance of the biblical message with what are in fact its human limitations."[7] Perseverance in truth requires a knowledge of history and of doctrinal development. Fundamentalism ignores history and development, and many of both the attacks as well as the exaggerations connected with Vatican I and its teaching on primacy and infallibility are rooted in an ignorance of history and of the development of doctrine.

My aim in writing this book has been to show that Vatican I is not an obstacle to the path of synodality so emphatically embraced by Pope Francis, nor does Vatican I proclaim a sovereign and absolute primacy outside of and above the bishops with a highly centralized governing of all church life. The primacy and infallibility decrees do not preclude the collegial exercise of the primacy as it is more explicitly elaborated in Vatican Council II. History plainly shows that the petrine ministry has taken different forms at different periods of history. Pope John Paul, in the encyclical *Ut unum sint*, holds up the first millennium as a point of reference to show how the primacy could be exercised in the Church of the third millennium. Clearly the primacy of the first millennium, increasingly recognized and effective, did not involve a centralized government of the whole Church; the Pope did not appoint all bishops nor did he write any encyclicals. Mainstream theologians hold that in the first millennium, there are not more than two dogmatic definitions of doctrine apart from Councils, and these two were adopted by ecumenical councils. Thus the dogmatic definitions of Vatican Council I do not foreclose the collegial exercise of the primacy as more fully elaborated in Vatican Council II. The primacy

7. Pontifical Biblical Commission, *The Interpretation of the Bible in the Church* (Rome: Libreria Editrice Vaticana, 1995), 72.

and infallibility decrees of Vatican Council I provide a doctrinal landmark open to the path of synodality and to structures of communion, while safeguarding the need to provide for crisis situations where the petrine office can intervene with authority to preserve the Church in unity of faith and communion.

And so, the Church of the twenty-first century, as it embraces and learns from Vatican I, could greatly profit from Newman's penetrating insight:

"One cause of corruption in religion is the refusal to follow the course of doctrine as it moves on, and an obstinacy in the notions of the past."[8]

---

8. John Henry Newman, *An Essay on the Development of Christian Doctrine*, Part II, Chapter V, #8 (Westminster, MD: Christian Classics Inc., 1968), 177.

Other Titles of Interest

Gerhard Ludwig Muller
CATHOLIC DOGMATICS

For the Study and Practice of Theology

Dogmatic theology addresses the tension between God's self-communication and modern attempts to translate them into our own worldview and milieu.

Hardcover, 175 pages, 978-0-8245-2232-2

Paperback, 175 pages, 978-0-8245-2233-9

Robert P. Imbelli, Ed
HANDING ON THE FAITH

The Church's Mission and Challenge

Renowned theologian and teacher, Robert P. Imbelli, introduces the work of leading Catholic theologians, writers, and scholars to discuss the challenges of handing on the faith and to rethink the essential core of Catholic identity.

Paperback, 264 pages, 978-0-8245-2409-8

Eugene J. Fisher, Ph.D
Rabbi Leon Klenicki
Editors
THE SAINT FOR SHALOM

How Pope John Paul II Transformed Catholic-Jewish Relations
His Complete Texts of Jews, Judaism and the State of Israel 1979-2005

Pope John Paul II's efforts can serve as a model for reconciliation, inspiring both believers and non-believers to pursue deeper understanding and work together in harmony to help improve the world and achieve Shalom, the Hebrew word for Peace, wholeness and right-relationship, for all humankind.

Support your local bookstore or order directly from the publisher at www.crossroadpublishing.com

To request a catalog or to inquire about quantity orders, please e-mail sales@CrossroadPublishing.com